GHOST INVESTIGATOR

Volume 4:
New York & New Jersey

Written by

Linda Zimmermann

A Spirited Books Publication

To Molly, Boo! 10/04

Also by Linda Zimmermann

Bad Astronomy
Forging A Nation
Civil War Memories
Ghosts of Rockland County
Haunted Hudson Valley
More Haunted Hudson Valley
Haunted Hudson Valley III
A Funny Thing Happened on the Way to Gettysburg
Rockland County: Century of History
Mind Over Matter
Home Run
Ghost Investigator, Volume 1: Hauntings of the Hudson Valley
Ghost Investigator, Volume 2: From Gettysburg, PA to Lizzie Borden, AX
Ghost Investigator, Volume 3
Dead Center
Rockland County Scrapbook

The author is always looking for new ghost stories. If you would like to share a haunting experience go to:

www.ghostinvestigator.com

Or write to:

Linda Zimmermann
P.O. Box 192
Blooming Grove, NY 10914

Or send email to:
lindazim@frontiernet.net

Ghost Investigator: Volume 4
Copyright © 2004 Linda Zimmermann

ISBN: 0-9712326-6-0

CONTENTS

Author's Note

This has not been the best year of my life.

After what was supposed to be routine surgery, it was discovered that my dog, Shadow, had cancer. Shadow is a German Shepard mix, who began life as an abused and abandoned little pup. With lots of love (and doggie treats) he grew big and strong with two missions in life—protect us, and give us back a hundred times more love.

When I first heard the bad news, it was like everything crumbled inside of me and I felt hollow and empty. The last thing I wanted to do was write about death and ghosts. My days became consumed by trips to the animal oncology center for radiation and chemo treatments. The treatments are still continuing, and I'm pleased to say that Shadow has remained strong and happy. It's not an easy fight, this fight for life, but it is certainly one worth the effort.

What this experience has repeatedly emphasized, is that there are no guarantees in life. Terrible things happen, and you can either try to come to grips with them, or you can carry the bitterness, remorse and anger beyond your grave. The cases of hauntings that I investigate and write about invariably deal with those souls who have not yet released the negativity that resulted from the misfortunes life handed them. It's a lesson for everyone still breathing to take to heart—existence doesn't end at the lid of the casket, so live the best life you possibly can, and try to help others to do the same while you're at it.

For now, I still have my brave Shadow to guard me as I sit here and finish this book. And if the powers of medicine and love can triumph, he will be by my side for many more volumes to come.

Linda Zimmermann
August 19, 2004

Ghosts that Care and Ghosts that Smell

Tina was married in 1986, and she and her husband bought a house in Westwood, New Jersey. For the first year, the house underwent extensive renovations, and during that time the couple lived in the basement, which they had converted into an apartment with a full kitchen and bathroom. When the renovations were completed, the couple decided to continue living on the basement level, and rented the main portion of the house.

Tina often heard footsteps above her on the first floor, particularly in the kitchen, and naturally assumed it was her tenants. Turns out, there wasn't anything natural about it.

After having a son and a daughter, it was time to stop renting their house and move upstairs. That's when the trouble started. Tina continued to hear footsteps in the kitchen, but now that the tenants were gone, she discovered that the sounds of someone walking around occurred even when no one else was there!

Then the footsteps began on the staircase leading up to the second floor. Every night after she put the children to bed, there were clear and distinct sounds of someone climbing the stairs, and then moving to her son's and daughter's rooms. It was as if someone was checking in on the children. Tina kept checking on the sounds, and almost gave up hope of ever finding their source. Then one night, a solution presented itself—or herself, to be exact.

After hearing the footsteps going up the staircase yet again, Tina went to investigate. As she walked down the hall on the second floor, she suddenly felt a strong presence. Turning, Tina saw the figure of an older woman, perhaps in her sixties, at the other end of the hallway. The woman glowed with a bluish-gray light, and although at first she appeared to be standing, upon closer look, Tina realized that the apparition was floating just above the floor.

As if this ghostly manifestation wasn't enough, the figure began to move—very rapidly. The glowing woman rushed past Tina, buffeting her with an icy blast of wind.

"All the hair on my body stood up when she flew by me," Tina vividly recalls. "She went straight into my son's room and disappeared.

1

I began yelling that she had scared the heck out of me and she should never, ever do that again."

Of course, now that the ghost had shown herself, the question remained—who was she, and why was she there? Tina believes that she discovered at least part of the answer.

The previous owner of the house was a woman named Louise, who was in her sixties. She became very ill and was confined to the house for a long time. Finally succumbing to her illness, she died in that very house. Perhaps since life had robbed her of the chance to watch her own grandchildren grow up, she had chosen to watch over Tina's children?

Fortunately, Louise complied with Tina's request that she never show herself again, but she clearly did not vacate the premises. The footsteps in the kitchen and on the staircase continued on a regular basis. Also, the banister on the staircase had special lighting under the railing—perhaps Louise had been afraid of falling on the steps?—and often at night Tina would find that the lights were switched on, when no one had been near the switch.

For years this bizarre situation continued, but there were members of the family that still remained skeptical. Tina's brother-in-law thought nothing of volunteering one day to do some work alone in the basement, even though she warned him that he might hear strange noises. He simply did not believe the stories, and laughed at the ridiculous idea of there being ghosts in the house. When Tina returned home later that afternoon, her brother-in-law wasn't laughing anymore.

"He was standing outside, and he was as white as a sheet, trembling like a leaf," Tina said with some small satisfaction. "He told me he would never go back into that house alone again."

It seems that as he was working in the basement, he heard footsteps on the first floor that were loud, clear and unmistakable. Thinking that Tina must have returned home, he went upstairs, but found no one. Still not convinced that the footsteps were those of the ghost of a woman named Louise who had died in the house, he went back into the basement and continued working.

The second time he heard the footsteps overhead and found no one, he was a little less sure of himself. The third time it happened he was beginning to have serious doubts. The fourth time pushed him to the edge. The fifth time that the persistent spirit of Louise started walking around, his nerves snapped and he ran out of the house. The former skeptic had become a believer in a big way, and he refused to go back into the house until Tina came home.

"We've all been listening to your stories for six years," the man confessed to his sister-in-law, "but none of us ever believed you."

It was a hard lesson, but one this man will never forget.

Unfortunately, Tina's marriage fell apart and her husband moved out. Tina decided it was once again time for tenants, so she rented the basement apartment to two young women. That situation did not last long.

The women began complaining that items were being taken— small things such as jewelry, perfume and make-up. Tina allowed the girls to search the upstairs, but none of the items were ever found.

Then Tina noticed that one girl would go to the bar where her roommate worked, and would remain there until the bar closed at 2am. Only then, with her friend, would she go home. As she had a day job and had to get up early, the lack of sleep was beginning to take its toll.

After several weeks of this, Tina asked the girl why she always stayed out so late. With some reluctance, the girl finally confessed that she was terrified of being in that basement apartment alone. She kept hearing and seeing things she couldn't explain. These encounters became too much for her nerves to bear, and she moved out after just a few months. Her friend continued to put up with the sights, sounds and missing items for a while longer, but then Tina—now that she was a single mother—decided she needed to sell the house and find someplace smaller and more affordable.

It would be comforting, especially for the children, to move out of that haunted house and begin living under normal circumstances. Unfortunately, the phrase "Out of the frying pan and into the fire" was to become more appropriate than "Home Sweet Home."

Tina rented a small, one bedroom apartment in Paramus, New Jersey. The old building was on a dead end dirt road near an exit to the Garden State Parkway, and it wasn't in very good condition. She spent weeks using heavy-duty cleaners to scrub years of grime off of the floors and walls. Although the smell of these cleaning agents was strong, it was nothing compared to what was about to assault their noses.

One evening, Tina and her two children were in the living room watching television. Suddenly they heard the door to the apartment open. Then a nasty odor of sweat filled the room, and the rocking chair began moving back and forth as if someone was sitting in it.

"Oh no, we're going to go through this again!" Tina's daughter yelled in terror.

While Tina and her son had generally looked upon Louise's activities as more fascinating than frightening, her daughter had always been afraid. Whenever the subject of the haunting came up, she would cover her ears, not wanting to hear about it. So, when it became obvious that their new home was also haunted, her daughter was obviously not happy. To make matters worse, their smelly ghost had friends.

The way the entities entered the house was always the same—although the door on the porch never moved, the door into the apartment would swing open, and then the stench of body odor would permeate the air. Often the rocking chair would begin to rock. Tina and her children experienced this again and again, but noticed that the smell wasn't always the same. Over time, they were actually able to identify three distinct smells and came to believe that three entities with bad hygiene were haunting their place.

Another strange feature of the apartment was the huge open shower that could accommodate at least six or seven people.

"It was like the showers in a locker room," Tina said, "and when the door would open and those smells would enter the house, I used to say out loud, 'What's the matter, isn't the shower big enough for you guys?' "

Friends and family members who visited, would never return a second time. The three reeking apparitions were not shy about making themselves known to anyone. One day, one of Tina's friends was sitting with her in the kitchen, when the door opened. The porch was all enclosed in glass, so it could not have been the wind. Then the horrible smell filled the room.

"You know what?" her friend said, jumping to her feet. "I'm leaving now!"

The poor terrified woman never came back.

Tina didn't know most of her neighbors, and the ones with whom she did speak never mentioned any strange goings on. Of course, Tina never brought up the subject of ghosts either, as she didn't want anyone to think that she was crazy. However, she did strike up a conversation with a deliveryman who had worked in the area for many years. Although she didn't mention the smelly entities, she did ask about the history of the place, and got some startling answers.

The man told her that the land around them used to be a large celery farm. The building that was now rented out as apartments, used to house the farm workers—who at the end of a long, hot day, would return covered in all the sweat and grime of the fields!

While this seemed to explain who these ghosts were, it did not solve the mystery of why they kept returning to this place. Had the three men been killed in some farming accident? Had some other tragedy befallen them, perhaps inside the apartment? Or, had these men simply worked the farm for so many years that even after death they continued their old routines?

There may have been one benefit to having ghostly farmhands sticking around. When winter approached, Tina brought her rose bushes (there just happened to be three) into the kitchen. They continued to bloom throughout the winter, and in a most unusual way.

The bush with the red roses started blooming white. When the white flowers died, pink ones would return in their place. The other two bushes also had blooms that inexplicably kept changing colors, which had not occurred when they were outside in the garden. Just how a rose bush can change the color of its flowers, over and over, remains a mystery, but perhaps the three old farmhands had a little flower growing competition amongst themselves. Who knows how the energy from the other world can influence living things?

Much to the relief and delight of all the people who refused to step foot into to that apartment again, Tina and her children moved out after eight months. Fortunately, they were finally able to find a ghost-free home in a house that Tina and her new husband built in Orange County, New York. After experiencing so much, it's good to know that the children have nothing to worry about but typical teenage problems (which are scarier than most ghosts I know, if you ask me!), and that Tina has finally found a quiet and secure environment.

Hopefully, someday Louise will finally stop walking the floors and stairs of the house in Westwood where she died, and move on to a more peaceful place. Also, it would be comforting to know—for many different reasons—that the apartment in Paramus has undergone a spiritual "cleansing," and the farmhands have gone on to a more fragrant afterlife.

Will Tina or her children ever experience the paranormal again? Probably, as that is one door that once opened, is impossible to close forever.

Don't Touch That Grave Marker!

In October of 1998, Cheryl's sister bought a large Victorian home in Liberty, New York. Cheryl, her husband, Dan, and their four-year-old daughter, Aarron, moved into the second story of the house. The move was without incident, and they encountered only one unusual thing.

The previous owner "had left a lot of junk," according to Dan, and among the many items remaining in the basement was a grave marker. It was a small metal marker, something used temporarily at a fresh gravesite, until a permanent stone monument can be carved and set into place. The marker had been for a woman named Mary, who had died in 1978. Her last name did not match the name of the woman who sold the house, but obviously there must have been some connection. Although it was a strange discovery, the family had a lot of other things on their minds, so the marker was left on the shelf where they found it.

An infrared image of the closet where the woman appeared.

The winter passed quietly, with no sign that there was anything out of the ordinary in the house. Then in the spring of 1999, Aarron came running out of the playroom, yelling that there was a woman in the closet. Cheryl rushed into the room, but found no one. She repeatedly assured Aarron that there wasn't anyone in the playroom, but the girl refused to go back in the room for the rest of the day.

As time passed, Aarron would also talk about water running down the wall in one corner of the hall, insisting there was a steady stream plainly visible, but no one else ever saw it. Dan even went into the attic to check the area above that corner, and found that everything was dry. The young girl also complained about "lights" in her room at night that would keep her awake.

None of this seemed to be anything more than a child's imagination, until June of 1999, that is. Dan was cleaning the basement, and he innocently moved Mary's grave marker from where it had rested for decades. Then, to put it mildly, "all heck broke loose." The plumbing backed up and overflowed throughout the house, and despite Dan's best efforts (he is skilled in plumbing and carpentry), nothing seemed to solve the problems.

Cheryl began to joke that "Mary didn't like being moved," and that perhaps Dan should return her marker back to its original spot. He scoffed at the idea, and continued trying to find a rational fix to the rebellious plumbing. Then one day, just as suddenly as the problems began, everything was flowing smoothly again.

Relieved, and undoubtedly proud of her husband, Cheryl asked what new thing he had done to fix all of the pipes. Somewhat reluctantly, Dan admitted that he hadn't done anything else— anything other than move Mary's grave marker back to the exact location where he had found it! The inexplicable plumbing problems coinciding with the movement of the grave marker were enough to convince both of them that something from the other world was overflowing into their Liberty home.

Just in case they needed further evidence, another incident occurred a short time later. The family was eating dinner in the kitchen, and while they don't recall what they were talking about, they will never forget what happened. In the dish rack by the sink was a single item—a platter made of Corningware, which is known for its strength and durability. Suddenly, and for no apparent reason, the platter came up out of the rack and hit the floor, where it shattered into hundreds of tiny fragments. So much for strength and durability—but then you can't blame Corning, as their products are only tested under normal conditions, not paranormal.

Dan held up Mary's marker so I could photograph it.
I blotted out the last name to protect the family's privacy.

On another night, Aarron was at a friend's house, and Cheryl and Dan were watching television in the living room. It was quiet and peaceful, until a particular show came on—a show about haunted castles in Scotland. Then there was a very loud banging noise coming from the direction of their daughter's empty room. They didn't even get up to investigate, they simply said, "I guess Mary doesn't want us to watch this show," and changed the channel. Everything was quiet the rest of the night.

The family dog would naturally jump at such loud noises (especially when platters came out of dish racks and smashed to the floor). He also developed a habit of checking on Aarron every night after she went to bed, a habit he extended to Cheryl and Dan's son, Justin, after he was born. It was like the dog knew something strange was going on in the house, and just wanted to make sure the kids were okay each night.

This dog may have continued keeping an eye on the family—even after he passed away. Right after he died, Cheryl removed the dog's bowls, leash and all of his food from the house, as they were painful reminders of their loss. However, a month later, they came home to

The first floor shower.

find a small pile of dry dog food in the middle of the living room! Was this the dog's way of letting the family know that he was still with them?

Bizarre occurrences are not limited to the upstairs portion of this house. One evening, Cheryl's sister was taking a shower downstairs and the water turned icy cold. More frustrated than frightened, she called out, "Mary, I know you are just trying to be funny, but can I have my hot water back?" In the blink of an eye, the hot water returned.

There were also some problems with the valve, which began dispensing hot water when it was turned to "Cold" and cold water when it was turned over to the "Hot" position. Dan examined it and found that the pipes and valve had been correctly installed, so he assumed that the valve was defective. Removing it, he brought it to the local plumbing supplier, who could find nothing wrong with it. Dan decided to install a new valve anyway, yet the temperature reversal still continued. Then one day the valve corrected itself, with no help from human hands. Of course, it made absolutely no sense, but it is just one of the many inexplicable phenomena the family has learned to live with.

Unfortunately, other strange things happened to Cheryl's sister in that shower. On several occasions, she has heard children laughing and running up and down the stairs. At first, she assumed it was Cheryl's kids, but each time discovered that no one else was at home.

One afternoon she called Cheryl and was somewhat annoyed, wanting to know what had been going on upstairs all day, as for hours it sounded like the kids had been jumping up and down making a tremendous racket. Cheryl calmly replied that they had just gotten home, and the upstairs had been empty all day. It appears that if a woman's spirit does haunt the house, she has a few boisterous children to keep her company.

As disconcerting as it must be to hear phantom children, imagine what it must be like to actually *see* one—or worse yet, to be *touched* by a tiny hand reaching across the void between life and death. Unfortunately for Cheryl, the unthinkable did happen to her one day when she least expected it. She had just come home after dropping off her daughter and nieces at Girl Scouts. She carried Justin to the second floor, put him down on the couch in the living room, and turned to close the childproof gate at the top of the stairs.

Apparently, another gateway was open at the time, and at least one child had already slipped through, because there beside her was standing a blond little boy. He reached out his hand and quickly tapped her back as if playing a game of tag.

An icy jolt raced up Cheryl's back, and her hair literally stood on end. She could hardly believe her eyes, but there was a boy, as real and solid as a living child. And that touch of his hand—a solid touch, but not like anything from the world of the living. This contact with the dead had a stunning effect. Cheryl admits that she "freaked" and ran down the hall. She immediately called her father, and for half an hour he gently urged her to take deep breaths and try to calm down.

When Dan came home, Cheryl told him all about her unearthly encounter, and how the chill in her spine from the little boy's touch

An infrared image of Justin standing at the top of the stairs where the ghost of the little boy appeared. Justin's eyes seem to have their own spooky glow in the dark! (Aarron is standing to the left.)

was still with her. Despite all that had already occurred in the house, Dan kind of shrugged off the encounter, understandably finding it hard to believe that a dead child had materialized in his home, played tag with his wife and then vanished. However, he would undergo a very rapid change in attitude about one week later.

He and Cheryl were sitting in the kitchen, and he had a clear view of the hallway. As they spoke, he saw something move out of the corner of his eye, and turned to see a little boy run down the hall and turn into Justin's room. Dan told his wife what he just saw, and she said it couldn't have been Justin, as he was in the living room watching television. Determined to prove his wife wrong, Dan went into his son's room, but found that it was empty. Then he went into the living room and found Justin watching television, as he had been during the time some other little boy was running down the hall.

Another unusual manifestation occurred late one night in the living room (which always feels cold, even during the summer). Cheryl had fallen asleep on the couch, but something awakened her about 2am. There in the corner of the room was a wedding dress, floating in mid-air. Several times she closed her eyes and rubbed them, but each time when she opened them, the wedding dress was still there. She described the dress as a turn-of-century style with "poofy" sleeves, perhaps from the era when the house was first built. As she stared at the dress, wondering what else might appear or happen, it simply faded from sight.

The list of inexplicable events continues to this day. During Thanksgiving of 2002, another of Cheryl's sisters claimed to see strange lights moving around the downstairs' kitchen. The light fixture in the upstairs hallway periodically will not work. The childproof gate has opened by itself. One night a ball suddenly started rolling across the living room floor, prompting Dan to remark, "I guess the little boy wants to play." Many times when Cheryl is washing dishes or preparing dinner, she will turn to tell the kids to stop playing right behind her, but no one is there.

When Bob and I visited the house in March of 2004, there had been a quiet period of inactivity. After interviewing Cheryl and Dan, we set up some equipment and the video camera in the room where Aarron saw the woman in the closet. I also took a lot of infrared digital images with my new high-resolution camera. There was nothing unusual, so we moved on to the hall, the kitchen and all of the other rooms, except the living room, which we planned to do last, as the kids were watching television. There wasn't a single odd reading, sound or light. It seemed as if inactivity was the word for the day.

Next we went down into the basement, where Dan bravely risked Mary's ire by holding up her grave marker for me to photograph. (I would later feel guilty about it, but more on that later.) We examined

An infrared image of the corner of the living
room where the wedding dress appeared.

every corner of the extensive basement, but still there was nothing
unusual.

Then we went to the first floor, where Cheryl's sister told me all
about her experiences. I could find nothing unusual about the shower
area, or any of the rooms. However, as I walked down the central
hallway that connected all of the rooms and led to the stairs to the
second floor, the EMF meter started fluctuating. Setting up both
meters, I confirmed that there was some high level of energy in the
hallway, mostly concentrated between the kitchen and bathroom.
There suddenly was also a very strange and overpowering feeling, the
type that kind of grabs you in the throat and makes it difficult to draw
a breath. Fortunately, stepping away from the area relieved the feeling,
but any illusions of inactivity were shattered.

An infrared image of Dan standing in the first
floor hallway where there were high EMF readings.
The bathroom is at the end of the hall.

The last stop was the living room on the second floor. By this
point, I really didn't expect to catch anything on the cameras, so we
didn't bother to leave the room (which is normal practice, so as not to
disturb anything or make any noise). Cheryl, Dan, Bob and I were

chatting away as the video camera taped in infrared, in the direction of where the phantom wedding dress had appeared. We didn't see anything, or feel anything and after a few minutes decided to wrap up the investigation.

Over the course of the following week, I went over the digital images and found nothing unusual. Then I sat through almost all of the lengthy videotape, which as I have said in the past amounts to sitting and staring at a wall for hours—if nothing is happening. Nothing was happening, and I stopped near the end of the tape.

However, a couple of months later when I began to write this story, I went back to the video and decided to watch some of the tape to refresh my memory. I realized that I hadn't watched the living room footage and leaned back in my chair and prepared myself to be bored for a while. Suddenly, something caught my eye. It was a tiny white spot of light that zipped across the room in a flash. A minute later, there was another. Finally, there was something small and sparkling that slowly moved from the area where we were standing behind the camera, over to the corner where Cheryl had seen the wedding dress, where it disappeared from sight. At that point, thinking that there wasn't anything to see, I had shut off the camera.

If someone had been playing a game of tag with me, I was definitely "it."

As for Dan, things began to go haywire again after our visit. It's difficult to believe that just by moving the grave marker misfortune follows, but Dan was definitely batting a thousand in the bad luck department after touching Mary's marker. The next day, things started to go wrong around the house, most noticeably with his computer. Everyone else had no problem using it, but for some reason the computer refused to recognize any of Dan's passwords or user names. The problem persisted for weeks, despite tech support help from both the computer manufacturer and Internet provider. Everyone told him that nothing was wrong and there was no reason it shouldn't work, yet it didn't. Then one day the problem disappeared as suddenly as it had manifested.

When I began writing this story, I naturally had a lot of questions. Who were all these children, and why were their spirits still playing in this house? Why was there a grave marker in the house, what connection did it have to previous owners, and why did this woman's spirit get vindictive every time Dan moved the marker?

16

I called the local newspaper, the *Sullivan County Democrat*, and asked about obituary files from 1978. They have back issues on file, but I would have to arrange to go to the office to view them. They suggested I contact the local library, which I did and was pleased to find out that they would do a search for a small fee.

A week later, I had a copy of Mary's obituary in my hands. I called Dan that night and found out that one of the women listed as Mary's daughters, was the previous owner of the house, which explained why the grave marker was there. Also, I asked Dan if he knew where the cemetery was located that was mentioned in the article as Mary's final resting place (which may not actually be the case under the circumstances!), and it turned out he knew exactly where it was, because that cemetery was right across the street!

Does Mary leave her grave, cross the street, and enter the house, searching for her daughter? Does she get upset when she finds that her daughter is gone? Does she get angry when Dan moves her marker, afraid that it will be thrown away and she will be forgotten?

There are still many questions to be answered, but at least now we know Mary's connection to the house. Cheryl plans to continue the search for answers, hoping to find the reasons why their house is so haunted.

For the most part, the situation remains relatively quiet in this Liberty home—if you can call any level of ghostly activity quiet. Things still do occur, but nothing has smashed recently, and no solid manifestations of the dead have appeared to touch the living.

Dealing with the world of the paranormal is filled with uncertainties. However, I would wager that one thing is for certain— Dan does not plan to move Mary's grave marker ever again!

***

Timing is indeed everything. Within a minute of printing out the final version of this story, I checked my email and found a message from Cheryl, whom I hadn't heard from in weeks. Coincidence? Possibly, but as I was writing my conclusion that things were quiet in the house, she was sending me an email that proved this was no longer the case. The following is her email, and please note that "Mary's room" refers to the room in the basement where the grave marker is kept:

"On July 23rd, I had to go down into the basement (my favorite place) to our extra freezer that we keep down there. It was a rainy day and I really did not want to go down there but Dan was at work and the kids wanted lunch. I went to the back door to Dan's shop in the rain and attempted to open the door. We never have trouble opening this door but on this day I was out there for five minutes cursing everything but was unable to open it. I had no choice but to go through the door in my sister's house.

Well maybe I should have given up because I couldn't get that door open either. It took me I don't know how long to finally loosen it enough to squeeze through. After getting on the step and closing the door, a curtain rod that my sister had on one of the steps decided to scare the heck out of me by flying down the stairs. At this point I had a very hard time breathing. I'm not sure if it was nerves or what the feeling was, but I was extremely unnerved being down there alone.

The freezer, of course, is located right next to Mary's room, which just thrills me in general, but I try to ignore that. I finally made it to the freezer and do you know that I could not get that freezer unlocked for nothing! Maybe it was my nerves getting the best of me, but all you have to do is put the key in and press and turn. These are doors and locks that we never have trouble with normally. Needless to say I could not wait to get out of there and once I did, my breathing came back to normal but boy was I in a sweat. I ran back upstairs and called my father.

Yesterday I had to make another trip down there and I had absolutely no problem opening the back door and my breathing was calm. I have no explanation of what that was all about, but I am now keeping a log of what is going on. That was the first and only time that I have ever felt that nervous or actually frightened about any of this. What do you think?"

I replied to Cheryl that unfortunately, I think there may be things in that house that don't want her there.

This is definitely one of those stories to be continued…

Murder! Murder!

John Johnston was no good. He drank too much. People in Passaic County, New Jersey, who hired him for odd jobs, would find that he had stolen things from them. Then around Christmas of 1849, he went too far.

After a particularly heavy night of drinking, Johnston was feeling amorous. He got a ladder and tried to climb into a woman's bedroom window. He made such a racket in the attempt, people were awakened and he was apprehended. Johnston was later brought before Judge John Van Winkle of Hawthorne. The two men were well acquainted—Johnston had worked for the Van Winkles, who had treated him like their own son. Unfortunately, his drunkenness had brought an end to his employment, but still Johnston hoped that their previously warm relationship would be to his advantage in court.

However, instead of being released, Johnston was publicly admonished by Judge Van Winkle and given a sentence that he did not feel fit his alcohol-induced indiscretion. The judge insisted that Johnston should have known better and justice must be served. Johnston was overheard saying, "I'll get him for this."

Judge and Mrs. Van Winkle

19

In the early morning hours of January 9, 1850, the liquor-soaked brain of John Johnston drove him to get his revenge. Stealing a ladder from the Van Winkle's gristmill that stood behind the house, Johnston took precautions this time that he hadn't on his previous housebreaking attempt. Leaving his heavy boots (which he had stolen from a neighbor) in the snow, he silently climbed up the ladder in his stocking feet, and entered the north side of the house through an attic window.

The north end of the house as it looks today. The original attic window through which Johnston entered was removed.

None of the servants sleeping in rooms in the south part of the attic heard a thing as Johnston crept down the stairs. His objective was the judge's bedroom, but he suddenly made a slight detour.

The aroma of freshly baked mince pies lured him into the kitchen, where he calmly ate his fill. After all, who wants to commit murder on an empty stomach?

Johnston then proceeded to the bedroom where Judge Van Winkle and his wife, Jane, were sound asleep. Normally, the judge slept closest to the door, but the night before he hadn't felt well. He went to bed early, taking his wife's spot in bed, and then Jane later took his usual position by the door. In the darkness, Johnston probably didn't know of this sleeping rearrangement until his hatchet came down into the innocent woman's face and she began screaming.

Despite the fact that he had been particularly fond of the kind and generous Mrs. Van Winkle (to the point of calling her "mother"), he struck her repeatedly until she fell out of bed, bleeding profusely from horrible wounds. He then attacked the judge, who fought back as best he could after a terrible hatchet blow to the head. The carving knife Johnston also carried finished the cruel work, and then he fled.

The servants were roused by the judge's cries of, "Murder! Murder!" When the maid ran into the room, Mrs. Jane Van Winkle had only a few breaths left in her mutilated body, which lay on the floor in a deepening pool of her own blood. The sight of Judge Van Winkle was even more gruesome. Though still alive, the savage knife wound to his abdomen had caused his entrails to spill out onto the floor. However, despite the awful pain, the judge was able to name his attacker.

Immediately the word went out to locate Johnston. He was found at the Ridgewood train station, his clothes still wet with the blood of his two victims. He was brought back to the scene of his crime, where Judge Van Winkle found the strength to say, "Johnston, you are the man who murdered me. Why did you do this to me?" It must have been a remarkable and chilling encounter, but one that would not be repeated, as the judge followed his wife into death later that evening.

Johnston would not have much longer to live, either. After his conviction, he was sentenced to death. In Passaic County's first execution, John Johnston was hung on the gallows in Paterson, New Jersey, at the corner of Main and Oliver Streets. In a macabre case of poetic justice, the inexperienced hangman did not seat the noose properly to affect a quick death, and Johnston kicked and struggled in the air for a full five minutes before he finally died.

The shocking crime, sensational trial and ghastly execution left a deep impression on everyone involved.

This brutal double murder may have also left a lasting impression inside the Van Winkle house.

Ancestors of the Van Winkle family emigrated from Holland to America in 1639. In 1761, the judge's grandfather built a house by the

Goffle Brook, on land that is believed to have once been an Indian settlement, or perhaps a burial ground. The judge added a large stone addition in 1811. The extensive grounds also contained a very profitable gristmill powered by the brook. There were also various other buildings—including slave quarters. Over the course of many generations of Van Winkles, there appears to have been an inordinate amount of tragedies befalling family members connected with this property, not the least of which was the bloody double homicide.

A newspaper clipping from 1914. Although the image of the house is faded, the inscription is legible: "The Van Winkle Home on Goffel Road 1914 where the murder was committed."

According to a *New York Times* article on August 15, 1882, after the murders, "The end of the house where the murder was committed was locked and barred, and has been kept so ever since." The property was passed down through the family, although no other Van Winkles chose to live there. Instead, they appointed a caretaker and tried to rent the place.

However, no one wanted to live there for many decades after the brutal crime had been committed. Remarkably, a newspaper as prestigious as the *New York Times* reported that except for the caretaker, the place remained unoccupied as there was "no one seeming disposed to lease the valuable and beautiful property on account of the stories prevalent about its being the abode of unearthly visitants."

"Stories prevalent" of the Van Winkle house being the "abode of unearthly visitants!" These stories must indeed have been numerous and terrifying to keep people from living in such a beautiful house.

An early 20th century view of the Van Winkle house and the pond the judge had created for his mill on the Goffle Brook.

While it is not uncommon for murder victims' restless souls to continue to walk the earth seeking justice, revenge or sympathy, perhaps part of the reason why the Van Winkles' spirits clung to the house was that the murder scene was not cleaned up for over thirty years! When that section of the house was finally reopened in 1882, the *New York Times* described the gruesome murder scene that time and decay had made only more horrifying:

"A few days ago the long closed portion of the house was opened. The vines had grown so thickly around the doors and windows that a way was cleared with much difficulty. The hinges of the doors had rusted almost solid, and had to be pushed open by main force. The room had a damp smell, and everything was partially decayed: the furniture was almost hidden under dust, and there were masses of cobwebs in the corners. The aged couple had been murdered with a carving-knife and hatchet and as the fatal blows descended on their heads the blood spurted over the walls and on the bed clothing. The spots are still there, both on the half-rotted clothing and the faded walls."

Also, it was discovered that Mr. Johnston's means of escape had been left in the house: "The murderer made his escape through the garret, to which he climbed by a small ladder which he brought in for the purpose. The ladder was never removed; when the room was opened it lay in pieces on the floor under the garret scuttle hole."

It is inconceivable to think that the very clothes the Van Winkles were wearing when they were murdered had been left in the room, the blood soaked sheets and blankets had never been removed, and no one had wiped away the blood and gore from the walls! Why would anyone seal up a room in such a ghastly and shocking condition? Did the "unearthly visitants" arrive so soon after the murders that people were afraid to enter that room again, and so quickly locked it away from the world of the living?

A simple tip for anyone looking to rent or sell a property—if there's been a murder committed there, clean up the blood before you put it on the market!

In 1901, after the house was finally cleaned and restored, the property was sold, leaving the hands of the Van Winkle family for the first time in centuries. Curiously though, for the remainder of the twentieth century, some subsequent owners also experienced considerable misfortune. Regrettably for the house, trouble for the owners translated into neglect to the structure, which literally would threaten its very foundation by the turn of the new century.

In addition to the early accounts of ghostly activity, one member of a family that owned the house for sixty years recalls a couple of strange things. Megan Brennan, a teacher, is the granddaughter of Dr. and Mrs. Van Stone, who purchased the house during World War II. As a child growing up in the 1980s, Megan knew the story of the murders from an early age, and just accepted them as a part of the history of the house.

Most importantly, she never felt physically threatened in any way. To the contrary, she always "felt very safe" in the house, even though it had a distinct "presence." Indeed, if the spirits of the kindly judge and his wife do still linger, they should have no reason to be angry with the

Van Stones, or any other family who cared for and loved the old Van Winkle house.

The only place in the house where Megan ever experienced anything uncomfortable was the main staircase. Here, that "presence" was so strong it always felt as if someone was right behind her. Every time she had to go up those stairs, she would literally run. Her bedroom was the first room on the right on the second floor, and she would continue running right into her room and immediately turn on the light. Megan stressed the fact that she had no problem going into the basement alone to change a fuse if the lights went out, no problems at the actual murder site in the house, or anywhere else—just that staircase, which she continued to run up even after she had grown to adulthood.

The family cat also acted odd by that staircase. While the cat's behavior was perfectly normal everywhere else in the house, he would sit and stare at one particular area of the staircase—sometimes for hours at a time! This fixation lasted for all the years that the cat lived there, but since moving to a new house that behavior has never been repeated. There must have been something, or someone, around that staircase, but whatever it was remains a mystery.

The staircase where the presence was felt. (Photo courtesy of Don Smith.)

Perhaps it should just be termed a presence of unknown origin.

According to Megan, the only other problem with the old murder house was that none of her friends ever wanted to sleep over! Not that anyone could blame them...

Unfortunately, by the early twenty-first century, the unoccupied house faced demolition. Despite its eighteenth-century hand-hewn beams, its finely carved architectural details, magnificent fireplaces and 250 years of history, a developer planned to tear it down and build condos. Fortunately, there was one man who wasn't going to let that happen.

Henry Tuttman, a local contractor, bought the property in order to restore the home and preserve it for future generations. This was a major commitment, as the stone foundation was near collapse, all the electrical and plumbing had to be replaced, and termites had done their best to consume the rest of the historic building.

The cornerstone of the judge's addition to the house with the inscription from 1811.

Anyone who has updated or renovated even a single room knows the turmoil it causes. In this case, every room in the house is undergoing extensive renovations, so it would be understandable if no one noticed anything going bump in the night. Yet, despite the disorder and chaos, there have been a few unusual things worth noting.

There is a small bathroom on the second floor near the northwest corner of the house. Mr. Tuttman keeps the door to this bathroom closed, or at least he tries to. He has repeatedly found this door open after he has securely closed it.

His cat has taken a particular interest in this room, often sitting in front of the door and staring at it for long periods of time, much like the Brennan's cat with the staircase. There are now claw marks on the door as this cat has taken to scratching on it in his attempts to get inside. Even though there are a few thousand square feet of house for the cat to wander around, inexplicably he wants to get into this one tiny, nondescript bathroom—a bathroom that just happens to have a door that can open by itself.

The actual site of the murder as it looks today. The former bedroom is now an exercise and recreation room. (Photo courtesy of Don Smith.)

Even more convincing evidence that the haunting still continues occurred in January of 2004, when Mr. Tuttman suddenly woke up in the middle of the night. He didn't know what had awakened him, and he never had any trouble sleeping. However, for some reason, this night he simply could not get back to sleep.

Later that day, he was speaking with Don Smith, who is writing a history of the house, and mentioned that he was tired because his sleep had been disturbed. Don thought for a moment, and then realized that it was January 9, the anniversary date of the murders, and the time that Mr. Tuttman was awakened corresponded to the actual time of the attack!

The area of the attic where the murderer entered the house. The window is not the original. (Photo courtesy of Don Smith.)

When I visited the house in June of 2004, it was a warm, sunny morning—about as far removed as possible from the snowy dead of night in which the murders occurred. Still, there was a palpable sense of tragedy when standing on the spot where two innocent people were gored by a hatchet and carving knife.

Mr. Tuttman gave me a tour of the house, which was much larger than I expected, and Don Smith joined us to share his extensive knowledge of the people and events surrounding the property. I was nothing short of amazed by the effort and care Mr. Tuttman is putting into restoring this house, and I look forward to returning some day when the work is completed to see what will undoubtedly be an historic showpiece. I also wouldn't mind returning in the early morning hours of some ninth day of January and conducting an investigation…

Mr. Tuttman and I also discussed the possibility of an archaeological dig on the grounds to attempt to uncover traces of the past—possibly from the Van Winkles discarded trash and personal items, to artifacts from the slave quarters, to one of those infamous Indian burial grounds that so many fictional ghost stories can't seem to live without. There just might be some buried secrets to uncover in the earth that might help explain the long history of tragedies at this location.

For now, at least, the streak of bad luck seems to have been broken. The house is being returned to its former glory, the lives of its inhabitants are being researched and preserved, and if ghosts do still walk its halls, at least they don't appear to be too restless. In any event, I'm sure that this is one story that has more mysteries to be explored, and many more chapters yet to be written.

***

I would like to thank historian and writer Don Smith for bringing this house to my attention, and for providing the fascinating information and articles on the story of the murders and the history of the numerous other tragedies. While these tragic events may not reveal any evidence of ghostly activity, perhaps they may indicate that some unfortunate influence is at work here? As always, it's up to the reader to draw his own conclusions.

And as Don is the real expert on this subject, he was gracious enough to agree to write the following summary:

The Curse of the Van Winkles?

Arguably the greatest tragedy in the Van Winkle family occurred with the murder of Judge John S. Van Winkle and his wife on January 9th, 1850. However, the family's tragedies appear to have started around April of 1828, and it seems that their "curse" is still felt today.

Peter Van Winkle, the Judge's youngest son, died from a fall from a horse on April 29, 1828. Another of the Judge's sons, Cornelius, lost his own child, John Henry, on July 27, 1828. John Henry was only a year, five months, three weeks, and five days old.

Cornelius and his wife, Catherine, had another son they also named John Henry in 1846. He died April 6, 1851 at the age of five. Cornelius's surviving son, Simon, and his wife, Maria, had two daughters, Charity and Catherine. However, records show that Charity lived only from December 14, 1864 until 1866. Maria died in 1865. She was only in her early thirties. Simon's other daughter, Ann Maria went on to have two children, a daughter named Bertha and a son named Harold. The only thing that is recorded about them is that Harold died young. Just like his sister and cousins.

Zabriskie Van Houten (the Judge's great-grandson) was hit by a car in Caldwell, NJ, in 1934. He ended up with a fractured pelvis, cracked vertebrate and was in critical condition for long period of time. He was also married three times. He married his first wife, Addie in 1899. When she passed away, he married Addie's sister, Ruth—and she died July 27, 1931 (the same day Cornelius's first son, John Henry, died). However, it appears that things turned out well with his third wife, Inez.

Probably the most fascinating occurrence is what happened to Judge Van Winkle's granddaughter, Anna Elizabeth. She married Helmas Romaine, who had come from a wealthy family. He was estimated to be worth $500,000, and had no cares in the world. However on November 21, 1896, Romaine committed suicide by shooting himself in the side of the head.

It should be noted that even in death the Judge and his wife could not rest in peace. The Van Winkle family vault was located on what is now Pasadena Place in Hawthorne. In the vault, lay the Judge, his wife, and several other members of the family, but through time and wear, the front wooden door to the vault rotted off its hinges. People could look in and see the coffins. In fact, it became a "tourist stop" for people hiking through the woods up to Watchung Mountain.

On October 28, 1892, Anna Elizabeth removed the remains of the Van Winkles and had them placed in the Romaine Family plot in Cedar Lawn Cemetery. Ironically, they rest across from former Vice-President Garrett Hobart (under President William McKinley), who was the son-in-law of former Paterson mayor and lawyer Socrates Tuttle—the lawyer that defended John Johntson for the murder of Judge and Mrs. Van Winkle!

The Van Winkle family plot was destroyed. As for the Van Winkle homestead, it was handed down to Jennie Van Winkle (the Judge's great-granddaughter) and it was ultimately sold by her estate to Thomas Arnold around 1901. Thomas passed the house down to his son, Ivan Arnold. However, according to Jean Brennan (the daughter of later owners Doctor Claude and Dorothy Van Stone), the Arnolds for some odd reason abandoned the homestead.

"Calendars were left hanging on the wall, and dishes and clothes were left behind," said Mrs. Brennan. "What makes this really odd, is that the Arnolds moved to Glen Rock, just the next town over. They still paid the taxes on the property, but they abandoned it."

By 1942, the borough of Hawthorne had control of the house, and it was sold to Dr. Van Stone. When Dorothy Van Stone died in 1998, the house was left to her daughter Jean Brennan and her family.

"You have to understand, that we needed to make repairs and we had to take a second mortgage to do it," Jean Brennan said in an interview. "Ultimately my husband, Mark, lost his job with the recession (thanks to 9/11 also) and to make a long story short, we lost the house."

The Van Winkle homestead is now owned by Henry Tuttman, who is currently seeking to restore it to its finer days. But still, there does seem to be a pall on this house.

Unfortunately, there are no surviving members of the Judge's line of the Van Winkles.

***

Just before going to press, Don was researching the records of Johnston's trial, and came upon the actual transcript of the sentencing. In the midst of page after page of seemingly endless "legalese" was the following bizarre statement: "That John Johnston late of the township

31

of Manchester in the County of Passaic aforesaid laborer not having the fear of God before his eyes, but being moved and seduced by his mitigations of the devil...feloniously, willfully and of his malice aforethought...did make an assault..."

It seems remarkable from a modern perspective that actual court records would claim that the defendant was "seduced by the devil." Of course, even if the judge and jurors believed that this man was somehow possessed, it did not alter their final judgment. John Johnston was hung by his neck until dead, for the crime of murder.

What the records do not show is a crime far worse—that of sending two innocent souls into the realm of restless spirits...

Special thanks to Albert Stampone for his technical assistance with some of the photographs.

Ghost Magnets

It all began in 1982 when Judy's daughter, Ann, was about eighteen months old. Judy was living with her mother in Port Jervis, New York, and up to that point, they had never encountered anything unusual. Then the screaming began.

Little Ann would wake up in the middle of the night and her "blood-curdling screams" would send Judy running to see what was wrong. Something was terrifying her daughter, but she couldn't find the cause.

Then Judy began to notice that every morning she would wake up to find that her blankets were in a bunch down by her feet. She had never been a restless sleeper who kicked off bedcovers, and couldn't understand what was happening, until one night when she woke up because of a tugging feeling. There in the darkness, something was slowly pulling the covers off her. Quickly reaching for the switch behind her bed, when the light came on the pulling stopped. While there was no one to be seen, she sensed a male presence. Finally, reluctantly, she switched off the light, and almost immediately the covers began to be pulled off her again!

At the time, Judy was working two jobs, and was not in any mood for these paranormal tricks that deprived her of precious sleep. More aggravated than frightened, she shouted out, "Fine, you want to play your games, you just go right ahead and play your games! Ha, ha, ha, this is so funny! Go ahead, I don't care!" This outburst brought about a mixed reaction—from that night on, her daughter stopped screaming and slept peacefully, but unfortunately the game of cover pulling continued. Perhaps Judy should have been a little more forceful and direct in her admonition.

After putting up with the unwelcome night visitor for a couple of years, Judy got married and she and her daughter moved from her mother's house. Many years later when Ann was in her teens, she again spent the night there. She was awakened after midnight by a thunderstorm, and then heard the sound of someone shuffling up and down the hallway in slippers. The floor was not carpeted, so the sounds were very distinct and recognizable. Ann wondered why her grandmother was up walking around so late. In the morning when

Ann asked, her grandmother replied that she had slept straight through the night, not once waking up or getting out of bed!

Often during the day, if Ann was downstairs she would hear footsteps on the second floor, and if she was on the second floor, she would hear someone walking around downstairs. As nothing ever happened when Ann was not in the house, it was beginning to seem as though this girl was not only sensitive to spirits, her presence somehow attracted them like some type of ghost magnet.

After two generally uneventful years in Middletown, the family moved to a renovated summer home in Cuddebackville, where Judy said, "Things *really* began to get interesting." The first thing they noticed was that objects would disappear for days, sometimes months. Of course, everyone loses things, but these objects would reappear in the strangest places. For example, her husband Tom's glasses would be nowhere to be found, and then suddenly show up in the center of the floor.

Late one night, Judy awoke and felt one of her boys (they had two sons) climbing onto the foot of the bed. She assumed that one of them had a bad dream, and didn't realize that she was the one about to experience a nightmare. Although the child felt real and solid as he crawled up the bed between herself and her husband, he didn't feel quite "right." The weight and size was too big for her youngest boy, and too small for the oldest son. Looking down, she could see the depression in the covers the child was making, but the only problem was that there was no child!

As the phantom child crawled closer and closer, Judy feared that she was about to be physically attacked. She tried to scream her husband's name, but she was so scared that her voice caught in her throat. When the invisible child was just inches from her face, she heard a "whoosh", and a blast of cold air blew across her face. Then there was nothing.

In the morning, Judy told her husband that she knew who was haunting the house. When she declared that it was a child, her husband's only reaction was to ask if it had been a very small child. She replied that she believed it was and wanted to know why he thought that.

"Because last night a little boy climbed into bed and sat on my chest," he stated to her amazement. He went on to explain that he clearly felt the weight of the child but saw nothing, and was unable to move or speak until it was gone.

This little boy also liked to play with toys. One evening as Judy was doing dishes, her husband called her into the other room. There on the table was a little radio-controlled Snoopy on a skateboard. Snoopy was skating back and forth across the table, from edge to edge, almost as if a hand was pushing it back and forth. Neither her husband or son was holding the remote, but she suspected they had hidden it and were playing a joke.

"I said it was very clever, but that I would fix their little trick. So I went over to the skateboard, picked it up and took out the batteries. When I put it back on the table it continued to move back and forth! I then found the remote control, took the batteries out of that, but still Snoopy kept skating! We just couldn't believe it."

After several more minutes, the invisible boy must have finished playing, because the skateboard finally stopped. However, that was not the only toy to develop its own mysterious power. One night Judy heard a strange buzzing-type sound behind her. She looked to find a radio-controlled car on its side with the wheels spinning rapidly. Picking up the control box to turn it off, she found that it didn't have batteries. Reluctantly, she then picked up the car, and found that it, too, didn't have batteries. Yet there was the car in her hand, it wheels buzzing at high speed. Like the skateboard, the car eventually became still, but not before the hair on Judy's arms stood up and she became covered in goosebumps from the spine-tingling energy powering the toys.

Other tricks were not so amusing. The remote for the television was lost for months. One day when Judy was home alone and was cleaning the house, she found the remote and placed it on the center cushion of the couch. A short time later she went back to get it, and it was gone! She knew the ghostly prankster was behind the disappearance of the remote, and she was angry.

"That's it!" Judy shouted to the invisible little boy. "I want that remote returned. I'm leaving now to go shopping, and when I return I want that back here. This isn't funny anymore!"

When Judy returned from shopping, the remote was sitting in the middle of the stove. Judy thanked the boy, but then quickly added that he should never do that again. The scolding apparently worked, as they had no further problems with disappearing remotes.

Ann also had some frightening experiences in that house. Often at night she could hear the window curtains opening and closing. The curtains were hanging from round metal hooks, which made distinctive sounds as they slid back and forth on the metal curtain rod. These sounds were not the result of wind blowing the curtains, as this opening and closing would occur even when the window was closed tight. Ann refused to look at the window when she heard those sounds, afraid of what she might see looking in at her.

However, curtains were the least of the little girl's problems. One night, she was awakened by someone tapping on the side of her bed. Assuming it was one of her parents, she rolled over and opened her eyes. There, sitting by the foot of her bed, was a man dressed in green army fatigues, wearing a beret.

"I couldn't see his face," Ann explained, the passing of the years not having dulled the terror of that moment, "and I remember being scared out of my mind. And the most interesting thing about it was that he was sitting right *next* to the edge of my bed, but I was sleeping on the *top* bunk of a bunk bed."

The uniform appeared to be modern, and the soldier did not speak or make any motions. He simply sat in mid-air, looking at her, and Ann was certainly too frightened to say anything. It would have been fascinating to try to communicate with the military ghost, but you can't blame an eight-year-old for burying her head in the pillow and not opening her eyes again until morning.

There were some lighter moments in that house, as well, which helped to ease the tension. Returning home from shopping one evening, Judy hurried inside the house before Tom, and quickly turned all of the pictures on one wall upside down. Then she sat down at the desk and pretended to work on the receipts as if she didn't notice a thing. When her husband came inside and saw all the altered pictures, he "freaked out."

"I messed with him for about an hour," Judy recalled, laughing, "and then I confessed that it was me."

In 1990, the family moved out of that house, with its phantom little boy and soldier, and into a new home which they hoped would be quiet, peaceful and normal.

Not a chance.

Their new home, a 200-year-old farmhouse in the town of Greenville, was on a large piece of property, which also contained barns and the remains of the stone foundations of other buildings, such as a blacksmith's shop. The views are beautiful looking out across the hills, and there didn't appear to be anything spooky about the place—except maybe for the few graves down the hill in the local burial grounds.

Actually, things were relatively uneventful the first year or two after moving in. However, during that time there were major renovations taking place, so noises and confusion were commonplace. It was only after the work had been completed that the family began to notice that once again, they were not alone.

The first thing Judy noticed occurred when she thought she was alone in the house, sitting in the living room. (The living room is in the front of the house. There is an L-shaped hallway in the center leading to the right to Judy and Tom's bedroom. The stairs to the second floor are at the junction, and the kitchen is in the back of the house.) The kids were at school, her husband was at work, and there weren't any other houses nearby, so she wasn't expecting anyone. Suddenly, the back door opened and slammed shut, then heavy footsteps pounded across the kitchen floor and went up the stairs.

"Who the hell just walked into my house?" Judy recalled thinking as she ran upstairs after the intruder. "But I searched everywhere and no one was there. This happened many times over the years, we all hear the slamming door and footsteps."

Much of the activity in this house seems to center around the hallway. One night Tom and one of his sons, Mark, were watching television in the living room. Mark's attention was drawn to the hallway, and he looked over and saw someone standing there staring at him. Calling his father in a subdued voice and motioning for him to look, they both clearly saw a man wearing old farming-type clothes standing in the hall. When the unknown person realized that he had been seen, he ran into Tom and Judy's bedroom. Tom and his son ran down the hall after the man, but there was no one in the room. They searched everywhere. The only way a living, breathing man could have escaped was to vanish into thin air, in which case, it wasn't really a living man after all...

Another night, Judy, Tom and one of their sons heard the door to the basement being repeatedly opened and slammed shut very quickly. Once again, they ran to find out who it was, and found no one. The basement door was closed and locked—from the inside—so it could not have been anyone who had broken into the basement, and there wasn't anyone else inside the house.

Although much of the farmland in the area now contains houses, Tom and Judy still use their property to raise various animals, including goats. Every morning they have to get up early to milk the goats, which usually takes about an hour. One dark, pre-dawn morning Judy just didn't feel like getting up, so Tom said that he would take care of the milking by himself.

As Judy was enjoying her chance to linger in bed for another hour, she believed that she heard Tom come back in the house after only fifteen minutes. He then climbed into bed without uttering a word. In the dim light, Judy rolled over and looked at what she thought was her husband in bed next to her and asked what had happened, and why he came in so soon. He didn't reply and appeared to have already fallen asleep, so she decided to go back to sleep and find out what happened later.

She didn't have to wait long. After about an hour, she was awakened by the sound of the back door opening. It was now much lighter, and she could see that Tom was no longer in bed. A few moments later, he walked into the bedroom, and Judy asked what he had been doing. He looked puzzled, and said that he had been out milking the goats.

"But what were you doing 45 minutes ago?" she asked, thinking that she would finally get an explanation as to why he had come back to bed so soon.

"I was out milking the goats," he replied again.

"Didn't you come back in?" she asked, sitting bolt-upright.

"No, I was out the whole time milking the goats!" he repeated with more emphasis, wondering what his wife could be driving at.

"Then who was that in bed with me?" Judy asked in alarm.

"I'm sure I don't know!" Tom replied to a most unusual question for a woman to ask her husband.

It quickly became obvious that the man in bed with her hadn't been her husband. It also became apparent that it wasn't really a living man after all...

Fortunately, they have managed to deal with this ghost with a sense of humor. Sometimes when Judy asks her husband to fix something in the house he will reply, "Why don't you get your boyfriend to do it?"

They have even given the "boyfriend" a name—Sam, as the family who owned the farm for generations had a long line of men named Sam. So, if this is a former owner, the odds are good that they chose the right name, although from which generation and century remains to be seen.

Some things that can't be seen, but are nonetheless as plain as the noses on their faces, are the various scents in the house that have no rational explanation. The living room will often smell like tulips, daffodils and other fresh flowers, even in the middle of winter. The family will come home after having been gone all day, and open the door to the kitchen and be greeted by

One day Judy was outside of the barn with a baby goat in each arm. She was trying to push the bottom part of the door closed with her foot, but the latch was closed. Suddenly, the metal bar lifted out of the latch and the door swung closed. For a change, the bizarre activity was helpful.

the delectable aromas of brownies, cookies, cakes or pies. The flowers and baked goods clearly did not fit Sam's *modus operandi*, so they made some inquiries about the women who used to live there.

It seems that for much of the 20th century, a woman named Gladys was something of a family matriarch. In addition to helping to run the farm, she had a small side business—baking a variety of brownies, cookies, cakes and pies, and selling them to the locals who would gladly make the trip to her kitchen doorstep!

Although Gladys never made any physical appearances, they now believed they had two names to attach to the spirits that would regularly make themselves known in such an interesting variety of ways.

Even the family pets seem to be familiar with the ghostly residents, often reacting and interacting as if a person was there, when nothing could be seen by human eyes. One night their Doberman began growling, his hair standing on end, his stare fixed on one spot in the hallway where the figure of the man has been seen. The dog slowly moved to where Judy was sitting alone in the living room, putting himself between her and the invisible thing at which he was growling. This went on for almost an hour, which Judy admits really "creeped" her out. When her husband came home, whatever had been there must have vanished, because the dog returned to his normal playful behavior.

Unfortunately, the poor dog would be more severely traumatized one Christmas Eve. Ann was in bed, and she heard the dog enter her room. Usually, the dog would gently nuzzle her, waiting for permission to get onto the bed. This night, however, he wasn't waiting for an invitation. The dog leaped onto the bed, crawled under the covers down to her feet and huddled against her, growling and trembling uncontrollably. Ann had never seen the dog act that way, and she couldn't imagine what had frightened him.

Then out of the corner of her eye, she thought she saw something. Turning to look, Ann saw an oval-shaped, white light hovering in her doorway. Rather than being scared, though, she felt a very calming sensation, and she said, "Okay, you're here, just don't bother anyone." The light remained in the doorway, so Ann just turned her back to it and hoped it would eventually just go away. It must have, as the dog recovered and she went back to sleep.

As bizarre as this episode was, it is curious as to why the dog reacted with such terror to a presence that Ann felt was so soothing. Could something else in the house have scared the dog, and this second entity arrived to intervene and protect them? It's anybody's guess, but Dobermans are certainly not known for being easily frightened.

It's always interesting to try to establish some pattern to the paranormal activity at a specific location, as this may help explain the reasons behind it. In the case of this house in Greenville, the most active periods seem to occur around the beginnings of the spring and fall seasons. With such a wide range, at first this doesn't appear to be very significant. However, consider that for generations this place was the center a large farm, and the busiest times were during spring planting and autumn harvesting. If the spirits who reside here once

Ann (with her face obscured to protect her privacy) in her former bedroom. Mike Worden is in the background scanning the room with his EMF meter.

worked on that farm, then it actually makes some sense that there might be more activity at these times when in life they were accustomed to expending more energy.

The family also noticed another clear shift in the paranormal energy levels—when Ann moved out. Activity immediately decreased sharply, and remained well below what they had all been experiencing for the many years that she lived there. As with her grandmother's house when she was a child, it looked as though Ann was something of a lightning rod for paranormal activity.

For over a year, things were relatively quiet, but then some relatives seemed to get the paranormal ball rolling again. There was a wedding held on the property, and many descendants of the original family which owned the farm were in attendance. Apparently, the presence of so many blood relatives stirred up the dormant spirits and they were up to their old tricks, as well as some new ones.

The strange sounds returned. Then Judy saw an oval light in the corner of her bedroom. The last straw was when the faucet in the kitchen suddenly turned itself on full force. That was the day Judy decided to write me a letter and share the family's long history of ghostly encounters.

In November of 2003, Bob, police officer Mike Worden, and I visited the house, and our investigation got off to a bang—literally! We were all sitting in the kitchen as I interviewed the family, recording the conversation on tape. As they started to tell me about a shadowy figure they have seen passing by the window behind me, Bob interjected that he just saw someone outside, and then there were two very loud gunshots!

It was clear that someone had fired a high-powered rifle within just a few yards of the house, and for a very tense moment we weren't sure if the man was firing at us! I have been in many potentially dangerous situations over the years during my ghost investigations, but I have never had to duck before to dodge bullets. At least Mike was with us, and as he had just come off duty, it was comforting to know that if some lunatic was outside shooting at us, we had a cop inside who could shoot back!

Fortunately, Judy's son had seen the entire incident and we were not the targets. A hunter was driving by in his pickup truck, saw some deer in a field across the street, stopped right in front of the house and started shooting at them. Not only is this illegal, but I can't think of anything more despicable than killing innocent animals for fun. Fortunately, this lowlife's aim was as poor as his judgment (there was a row of houses in the line of fire on the other side of the field), and the deer safely scattered. But I had better stop here about expressing my opinion of such people, or I'll never get back to the story.

Judy called the police and gave them a description of the truck. A few minutes later, the police followed Tom into the driveway as he drove up in his pickup (which was actually the same model truck), but after a brief explanation the situation was resolved. I don't know if they ever caught the man, but the interlude certainly added a new level of experience to my investigations. (Although there was police involvement at the Lizzie Borden house, there were no shots fired. See *Ghost Investigator, Volume 2*.) Once the excitement had died down, so to speak, it was time to get back to the subject of ghosts—with a significantly heightened sense of awareness, I might add.

Judy continued by telling us about the time she was sitting outside by the back screen door. No one else was at home, but she thought she heard someone inside whispering her name. As she looked up, she clearly heard her name being called again in low, raspy voice, as a shadowy figure passed by the door, on the inside! "Oh great," she thought at the time, "now he knows my name."

This mysterious figure is not limited to the house and kitchen window. One day when Judy was in a small barn milking the goats, she heard the dogs and geese making a racket, just as they did when there was a visitor. Then a shadow passed over her, as if a person had walked by the window. Jumping up, she ran outside to see who was prowling around.

"All the animals were stirred up, so they definitely saw something," Judy recalled. "And something big enough and solid enough to block the light went by that window. But there just wasn't anyone there."

There is a basement in this house, but no one ever goes down there. There are also two crawlspace-type attics. No one has gone up into one of them, but in the other Ann found a letter (possibly from Gladys, as it was signed with her initials) to one of the family members named Sam. It was written in December of 1906, and although the handwriting was attractive, the spelling and grammar were quite poor. The gist of the letter was that the writer would probably be unable to visit Sam on New Year's Day, as she had caught a cold "standing in the hall Christmas night." Why she would be standing in the hall is anybody's

The barn window, by which passed a dark shadow.

guess, but I was reminded of Ann's experience with the oval light at her doorway on Christmas Eve. While the letter didn't contain any startling evidence, it nonetheless felt strange to be holding a letter that might have been written and received by two people who's spirits had not yet left the building.

At this point, our investigation was about to get underway, and I turned off the tape recorder, making a final comment that, "Hopefully I won't be needing to record anymore rifle shots."

The first task for the meters was not the hallway, living room or basement—it was Ann. Throughout her life, electronic equipment would often not function properly near her (during the entire interview, my tape recorder had a constant buzzing and ticking), and she had encountered an inordinate number of very close lightning strikes. It was something of a family joke that she was electrically charged, and no one wanted to stand near her during a thunderstorm.

There does appear to be some correlation between the intensity of a person's electrical field (everyone has one) and their sensitivity in what is referred to as the sixth sense. Ann had previously made the needle of a battery tester move by holding a lead in each hand, something no other family member could duplicate. I set my most sensitive electromagnetic field meter near her and asked her to remain perfectly still, as movement can generate a detectable field. After numerous readings, adjustments and more readings, it was clear that Ann does indeed possess an electrical field many times stronger than the average person. Perhaps in some way, this makes her a better antenna for the spiritual world.

Besides Ann, another place we found significantly high EMF readings was outside by the stone foundation of the old smithy shop. The closest source of natural electricity was from a transformer on the road, but it stood at a significant distance, and didn't appear to be a likely source of the readings. Of course, the ruins of an old smithy shop that never even had electricity wasn't a likely source, either, so this also remains a mystery.

There were some brief, but unusual readings in the living room. I may have disregarded them, but Bob took a picture of me at that moment and there are a few of those pesky orbs by my feet. As I have so often said in the past, I'm not convinced that orbs are anything paranormal, but when they appear at a moment when the EMF meter is getting high readings, I do take notice.

In the living room with an orb at my feet, and a similar orb near the dog.

There wasn't anything showing up in infrared—until we came to the attic. The opening in the ceiling was tiny, and as no one had been in that attic for decades, there was no guarantee that it would be safe to walk in (in other words, I didn't want to fall through a ceiling somewhere), so I decided against going in there. However, we came up with the next best thing.

Mike put the video camera on a tripod, then raised it up into the attic like a periscope, with the monitor screen aimed down so we could watch—"remote viewing" we called it. Even in total darkness, the infrared camera was clearly able to see the old hand-hewn beams that had stood the test of time. As we were admiring the craftsmanship, it looked like a little speck of light darted past the field of view. It was hard be sure as we were looking at a tiny screen six feet above us, but after a few minutes of taping, we played back the footage on the television, and sure enough, there were several of those mysterious points of light moving at various speeds and directions.

Mike using the video camera like a periscope to view the attic.

There had never been any odd occurrences connected with the attic, but Tom recalled that this section of the house was constructed with some very unusual building materials. A long time ago there had been a terrible train accident, with fatalities, and the cars had been wrecked beyond repair. However, some of the wood comprising the train cars was salvaged, and that was what was used to build this section of the house and attic.

Not exactly a smoking gun, but it was interesting to learn of the tragic history behind the wood that went into the area of the house that was displaying inexplicable spots of light moving about.

While there were no loud footsteps, shadowy figures or slamming doors during our investigation, there nonetheless were some tantalizing hints of what exists within those walls, and indeed, on the rest of the property.

The attic, with some orbs to the right.

I recently spoke with Judy to see if anything had happened in the nine months since we had conducted the investigation. Apparently, things quieted down, and remained relatively peaceful as they had when Ann first moved out. Ann has had a few strange experiences at her new apartment—but ghost magnets have to expect that kind of thing!

This old farm in Greenville may be peaceful at the moment, but I doubt with its varied and substantial history of paranormal activity that Sam or Gladys, or any other spirits, have moved on. They are most likely quietly going about their business, which apparently they think still involves running the farm. And if it is this family's fate to live in haunted places, at least these ghosts are relatively easy to live with. However, when you are in the ghost business long enough, you know that can change in one terrifying heartbeat...

Close-up of the bright spot.

Ann in the living room (standing where I was when the orb appeared), with is a strange blob of light behind her by the picture frame. There is no glass in the frame, so this is not a reflection. It is also much brighter and more solid than any orbs.

Riverfront Haunting

In 1872, a bridge across the Delaware River was completed, connecting Port Jervis, New York, with Matamoras, Pennsylvania. Anyone wishing to cross this bridge had to pay a toll, and the small tollhouse was on the Port Jervis side of the bridge. Although this original bridge was destroyed by ice just a few years later, it was rebuilt, and the tollhouse continued in operation until 1922.

An early view of the bridge and tollhouse.

Over the years, the little tollhouse grew into a series of interconnected buildings along Pike Street, where money was collected for more than just crossing the bridge. For example, there allegedly was a brothel, apparently catering to not-so-weary travelers. During Prohibition, the place supposedly served as a "Tea House"—the polite name for a speakeasy that served bootleg liquor in teacups.

In 1929, a new era was to dawn on the former tollhouse when a General Motors executive, Harold Dalrymple, purchased the place for his wife Florence, who along with her sister, Virginia, turned it into a restaurant named Flo-Jeans. In the days before the modern Route 84 highway, Route 6, which passed over the bridge, was a major thoroughfare in the region, and the restaurant became a popular spot for tourists. Among the notables who signed the guest book over the years were Governor Dewey, Joe DiMaggio, Lady Bird Johnson and actresses Irene Dunne and Gloria Swanson.

An original "Rate Of Toll" sign. A "Man and Horse" was charged 7 cents to cross, cows were 3 cents each, and a "Score of Sheep or Hogs" was 20 cents.

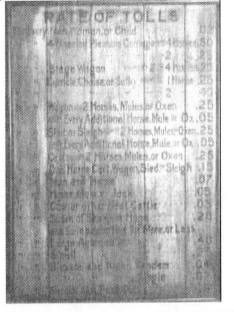

Virginia died in the 1950s, but Florence remained devoted to her restaurant for the rest of her long life. Even when she was old and could barely see, she had a young man to escort her to the door to welcome the regulars. In addition to the great food, there was always something new to see in Florence's large doll collection that filled the dining areas. This collection began decades earlier on Mother's Day in 1929, when Harold gave his wife (who had no children of her own) a doll. From that point, Mother's Day became a very special time in their lives, and a very special event at the restaurant.

Florence died in 1983, and her nephew tried to keep the restaurant running. Unfortunately, times had changed and the glory days of Flo-Jeans were gone. Unable to pay the taxes, Flo-Jeans went out of business in 1985 after 56 years in operation. For three years everything was left exactly where it stood the night they closed their doors. Then in 1988 the property went up for auction. Lynn Wallace, who remembered the place from her childhood when she would visit her grandparents in the area,

A vintage Mother's Day poster reading "Enjoy Dinner With Us."

50

A postcard showing the main lobby with some of Flo's doll collection.

thought it would be a shame to lose such a landmark, and she decided to take a look at the famous restaurant and see if it could be revived.

"It was very bizarre walking in there," Lynn recalls. "The restaurant had closed right after Valentine's Day, and the tables were still set and decorated with hearts. There were even plates of heart-shaped desserts that had dried and turned black over the years."

In addition to three-year-old groceries in the kitchen and storage areas, there was three years worth of neglected maintenance to the buildings. It would take a lot of work to clean and repair, but it was a project Lynn was willing to undertake. She put in a successful bid, and soon became the new owner of the historic tollhouse and restaurant— and *everything* that was included, both what could be seen, and what could not.

It took about a year to get the place ready to open, and during that time there were some clear signs that the buildings were not totally unoccupied. Objects that were left in one spot after work was completed at night, would often be found to have been moved when they returned in the morning. They would also frequently hear footsteps (especially on the second floor when everyone was downstairs) and strange noises that usually began after nightfall.

51

Though it was all "very creepy," it didn't appear to be anything to be overly concerned about, and a few moving objects and odd sounds certainly wouldn't keep them from opening in time for Mother's Day...

The old tollhouse section of the restaurant from a postcard.

About a week before the scheduled grand opening, Lynn was busy with last-minute preparations. A pair of French doors had been installed by the front entrance, and they had recently been varnished. Lynn was using a scraper to remove spots of the varnish from the glass, when the scraper came out of her hand. It went up in the air, and came down right on her wrist, where the razor-sharp blade hit with such force that it severed an artery, three tendons and several nerves.

Although she knew she was badly hurt, like a good restaurateur, Lynn's first concern was the new carpeting, so she quickly grabbed a drop cloth and wrapped it around her wrist, which was spurting blood. Fortunately, there were several other people in the building, and her brother rushed her to the hospital. However, she had lost a dangerous amount of blood, and the damage was so severe that they had to transport her to a better-equipped hospital. Although she recovered, she did lose some movement in that hand. And needless to say, they did not open Flo-Jeans in time for Mother's Day.

If someone or something didn't want "strangers" in Florence's place on *her* special day, they certainly had a terrible way of showing it. When I asked Lynn about how the scraper managed to come out of her hand in such a manner, she really couldn't explain it. Obviously, dropping a tool is nothing out of the ordinary. However, having one flip out of your hand and then strike your wrist in a blow powerful enough to sever tendons is another story—and in this case not one that had a happy ending.

Fortunately, the restaurant opened a few weeks later, after Mother's Day, and things went well. Then in November, Lynn was on a ladder.

"I don't remember losing my balance, but all of a sudden I was falling fast. And I still can't figure out how I managed to hit the floor head-first."

This accident required several stitches in her head. There were to be other strange accidents, as well, the results of which all seemed to go beyond the actual circumstances.

"I'm not a clumsy person," Lynn explains. "I've never been accident-prone, and these things never happened to me anywhere else."

Florence and Harold.

Fortunately, after a year or so, the place seemed to "accept" her, and there were no more serious accidents. However, while the injuries ceased, the strange events did not. One waitress felt a presence in the front hallway (where Florence would greet guests) and saw a figure. Most of the staff were unwilling to go into the basement laundry room alone, as they would feel a strong presence and hear noises. Extra lighting in the basement was installed to give a greater sense of security.

Over the years, Lynn and the staff just came to accept that the place was haunted, and while it's something you can never quite get used to, people do actually learn to live with the unknown—just as long as the unknown isn't trying to hurt you, of course.

My husband, Bob, fellow ghost hunter Mike Worden, and I investigated Flo-Jeans one night in November of 2003. As Mike had grown up in Port Jervis, he was familiar with the restaurant, but for Bob and I it was our first visit. Regardless, we were all amazed at the sheer size of the place and the maze of rooms on so many different levels that is was very difficult to get your bearings.

While Mike and Bob prepared the equipment, I sat with Lynn in the dining area by the main entrance and asked questions about the history of Flo-Jeans. She said that many "old-timers" had visited over the years and shared their interesting memories of the place. Several had mentioned that the restaurant had been damaged by fire, but Lynn was unable to find any proof of that.

Just at this point in the interview, there was a very loud cracking noise behind us, clearly picked up on the tape recorder. Startled by the sharp sound, I asked, "What was that?"

"That was the fire," Lynn replied with an odd look as she pointed to the burning logs in the fireplace near the bar.

Of course, burning wood makes noise, but the timing of this very loud crack—coinciding with Lynn talking about a damaging fire at some point on the restaurant's history—certainly caught my attention. As that was the one and only loud sound from the fireplace that night, and as I am often hesitant to chalk up anything to coincidence in a haunted location, I will just label this crackling fire as suspicious!

There would be plenty of other things to be suspicious about that night, too. As we arrived, the baseboard heater in the front hallway by the entrance began to make a banging noise, as if it was being struck by a metal object. Again, such heaters can make noises, but this was a persistent, rhythmic banging that Lynn said she had never heard before, and it seemed to bang more rapidly every time we entered the hall.

"You guys are stirring everything up!" she exclaimed smiling, but nonetheless hoping that we wouldn't have too much of an effect.

There were some strange readings around the piano in the old tollhouse section of the building. There was also an odd feeling there—

more of an impression than a presence, but nothing I could put my finger on, and nothing that was captured on any photographs or video.

The fireplace near the bar, from a postcard circa 1960s.

We then went upstairs to the locker and storage rooms that once served as the brothel. There wasn't anything out of the ordinary that our instruments could detect. After a while, Mike went downstairs, and Bob and I remained to take a few more pictures. Suddenly there was a tremendous crashing sound as if something heavy had fallen, like a person hitting the floor. Bob and I thought the sound had originated from downstairs, and we called to Mike to see if he was okay. He was fine, but he wanted to know if we were okay because he just heard the same loud noise—only he thought it came from upstairs where we were!

Only the distance of the flight of steps separated us, and we all agreed that the sound did not come from the staircase itself. Yet how could such a loud crashing sound appear to come from two floors at the same time, and why wasn't anything found to be out of place? Another thing to chalk up to suspicious circumstances. It looked like I was going to be needing a lot of chalk!

Lynn continued our tour of the enormous facility, next taking us to the private rooms that once served as a residence for Florence and her husband. The "pink room" that was their bedroom definitely had what can only be described as a creepy feeling. As we stood there, while

Lynn talked about Florence, a rose fell from an old silk flower arrangement sitting on a shelf, and landed at our feet. Once again, this was not solid evidence of ghosts, but the timing was—you guessed it—suspicious.

Looking down a staircase toward the main dining room, which stretches along the river. Note the bright spot near the top, center of the photo.

Then there was the banquet room door that would not close. Lynn repeatedly tried to pull it closed, but it wouldn't budge into the doorframe—something that had never happened before. At another door that we found locked, Lynn took out her keys and was moving to unlock it, when the key chain fell apart and her keys scattered across the floor. However, rather than be deterred by these little mishaps, we were only further encouraged to continue the investigation.

The basement was an imposing series of rooms, with an interesting mixture of modern items and relics from the past. The most curious, and disturbing, item was the large, stainless steel embalming table. Lynn has no idea why the table was being stored in the basement, so there is no way to know if it was ever used for human bodies. Regardless, it was definitely not the type of thing you want to encounter in the dark!

What was curious by their absence in the basement (and indeed throughout the restaurant) were those darting or floating white lights we often see on the infrared video at haunted locations. I'm still not entirely convinced that many of those mysterious objects aren't clumps of dust or airborne particles. However, if that were the case, then surely in the basement or storage rooms we would have stirred up enough particles to create an infrared snowstorm. Yet, with both Bob and Mike taping with two video cameras from top to bottom and from end to end of Flo-Jeans, there wasn't so much as one unusual speck. Just when you think you have a rational explanation for something…

Mike did have a strong feeling that someone was behind him near the laundry room, but other than that, our basement investigation did not yield any results. When we came back upstairs, Mike again experienced the sensation of a presence, and it occurred near a particularly large boy doll. His EMF meter also registered high readings, and his digital camera refused to take pictures of that doll. The overall effect was quite disconcerting. (I confess that the next day I emailed Mike my picture of his "evil doll" friend to remind him of the experience!)

As the investigation was winding down, we went back to our equipment cases near the main entrance. The baseboard heater was still making a racket as Lynn went down that hall to turn off the lights in

Mike's favorite doll.

the men's room. When she returned, she said she had a strange feeling in there, and heard noises. We grabbed our gear and went to check it out. As I stepped inside the darkened restroom, for the first time that entire night I felt some fear. There was something very intense, oppressive and decidedly hostile.

Instinct told me to run, stubbornness and experience told me to go all the way inside and ask a the obvious question.

"Is anyone in here?" I asked, trying to sound authoritative.

The EMF meter suddenly spiked. I took that to mean, "Yes."

We spent several minutes photographing and recording the hall and bathroom, and while there were no more sounds (other than a distinct increase in the heater banging) or images, the feeling persisted. In fact, it grew until it was almost unbearable—and then it was gone. A second before it was so powerful our skin was crawling, and then just like that it didn't seem any different than any other bathroom.

It was an intense finale to a fascinating investigation, and it left me with the impression that there was more than the spirit of a sweet little old lady within these walls. Unfortunately, it is impossible to know all that has transpired over the long history of this former tollhouse, brothel, speakeasy and restaurant. Those who commit dark deeds seldom publicize them, but as so many cases have revealed, they do leave imprints and clues for future generations. However, for the most part, the unusual activity that takes place here seems to be nothing more than an attempt by the dead to remind the living that they have not yet left the building.

If you have an appetite for good food in an historic restaurant with great views of the Delaware River, then Flo-Jeans is definitely the place to go. And if you see shadowy figures, hear strange noises and feel a strong presence while you're there, don't worry. It's all part of a dining experience that's out of this world...

The hallway where the heater was banging. The men's room is on the right in the middle of the hall. Newspaper stories about the history of the restaurant cover the wall on the left.

Looking down the hall in the other direction--A bright spot of light appeared near the ceiling.

The Restless Cemetery

There is an old cemetery in Stony Point, New York, where resting in peace does not appear to be on the eternal agenda.

In August of 2003, Sara Gonzalez sent me an email describing a few haunted sites she had visited with a group of young ghost hunters. One of them that caught my eye was this cemetery, which was supposed to contain the graves of several witches put to death in the 1700s. In all my years of research into Rockland County history, I had never heard of a single instance of any suspected witches being killed. In fact, the only reference to any witch was the trial of Naut Kaniff in West Nyack in 1816 (see my book *Rockland County Scrapbook*, page 56). Still, if there was any grave marker in existence in Rockland that even mentioned witches, it was worth a trip just for that.

Mike Worden and I arranged to meet the ghost hunting group at the cemetery one warm and humid evening. We arrived a little early, and decided to check the equipment before beginning our investigation. Curiously, I found that my tape recorder was already running, and had been recording for about ten minutes. I suppose it could have bumped against something in the equipment bag on the ride down and turned itself on, but to record, you have to press a small record button and the large play button simultaneously, which on this unit would be extremely difficult to do by accident.

I listened to the recorded portion of the tape and only heard muffled voices, which I believe must have been those of Mike and I as we drove to the cemetery. While it isn't anything I can ascribe to the paranormal, it was odd, and something that had never happened before in all my years of hauling around bags of gear under considerably less than gentle conditions. However, things were to get even stranger with the tape recorder.

The group arrived, consisting of Jesse Beyea, Jim and Tom Zorn, Nick, Christina and Sara Gonzalez. They began giving us a tour of the more active places in the cemetery, describing things they had witnessed and photographed—including some things that looked neither human nor animal.

When we reached the back portion of the cemetery, where the witches were allegedly buried (we never found any), I tested the tape recorder with a few words. When I played it back, there was an additional voice that was not mine. I played the mysterious words back for everyone and they all agreed as to what the voice was saying, and they did not think that it was the voice of anyone in our group.

A fallen gravestone in the area where legend claims witches are buried. There is an orb on the upper right edge of the photo.

However, I am not convinced. I would rather not write the words here as they are kind of silly, and I tend to think the voice sounds like Mike's. As he was standing at least twenty feet away at the time, perhaps the distance, and cutting off part of his words, produced the strange sentence. I am the only one who believes this is the real explanation for the bizarre recording, but even though I'm outnumbered, I have to state my case. However, what happened next left no doubt in my mind as to the nature of the event, or the ghostly cause...

In that same spot, just moments later, the EMF meter registered high readings. The cemetery has no power lines or any natural sources of electricity, so the meter should have displayed nothing but zeroes.

Simultaneously, the brand new batteries that Mike had put in his tape recorder went dead. One of the group's camcorder batteries was suddenly completely drained, another had its power drop by half, while someone's cell phone battery charge decreased significantly.

As if that wasn't enough, the infrared thermometers registered an instant drop in temperature from 76 degrees to 56 degrees, although it felt even much colder than that. A few people smelled the faint odor of smoke, and one girl claimed that someone touched her shoulder. All of this occurred in rapid-fire succession in the span of just a few seconds. It was intense, and it was unmistakable: there was *something* in that cemetery.

The area where all of the batteries were drained, and where the unusual voice was recorded. The bright spots in the background are a pair of reflectors on a tree. There are numerous orbs, but there were also many lightning bugs.

Unfortunately, the infrared camcorders could not provide any reliable evidence. To be sure, there were spots and streaks of light around us—but on an August night near the woods, there were so many lightning bugs, moths and all manner of flying insects that at times it appeared as if we were photographing a snowstorm. I did capture a few orbs on the regular camera, but again, with so much insect activity in the air, it was not definitive proof.

Something else very curious happened—as we were walking back along the path toward the parking lot, my camcorder was picking up a flurry of tiny spots around my feet. Mike's camcorder did not record them, and we also couldn't see anything with the flashlights.

As darkness had already fallen, and we did not want to invite a visit from the police (they regularly escort people out of the cemetery at night, so please always respect the rules), we packed up our gear—making sure the tape recorder wasn't touching anything else—and headed out.

I recently contacted Sara for an update, and she informed me that the group is still encountering strange things at this cemetery. In a way, it is unfortunate to continue to receive accounts such as this, as so many people hope that death will bring them lasting peace. This cemetery is just further proof that resolving your problems in life will spare you a lot of trouble after you die.

Mike took this photo of me in the "cold spot." Nothing unusual appeared (I assume that was a living person's hand!), but it reminded me that you never know what's behind your back at a haunted site...

The Old '76 House: Echoes of History

Early 20th century postcard of the '76 House.

By the time Casparus Mabie began building his house on Main Street in 1753, Tappan was already an old town. The grant for a township had been issued in 1686, by 1691 there was a courthouse, and a church was built in 1694. Tappan was an important center in early colonial days, and Mabie's house would play an important role in the coming Revolution. Patriots would meet at the house to discuss the latest news and share information, and it came to be known as the "listening post." However, its most famous role would be as a jail, when British Major John André was held there for his trial and execution.

In September of 1780, Major André received the plans for West Point from the notorious American traitor, General Benedict Arnold. When the treasonous plot was uncovered, Arnold escaped to the safety of the British lines, but André was taken prisoner. He was brought to Tappan and held in Mabie's house. On September 29, Major André was put on trial at the Tappan church. The recommendation that the board of inquiry delivered to George Washington stated that this British officer caught in civilian clothes "ought to be considered as a spy from the enemy" and "ought to suffer death" as a consequence. Washington signed the death warrant and André's fate was sealed.

On October 2, André was taken from the Mabie house and led to the place of his execution. Ever the gentleman and brave soldier, he put the noose around his own neck, and tied a handkerchief over his eyes. As he had predicted, there was only a "momentary pang" as death was almost immediate, and his body was buried on the spot where he died.

The famous house became a tavern in 1800, and for most of the next two hundred years the "1776 House" continued to serve the public, becoming one of the country's oldest such establishments. Today, the fully restored and expanded Old '76 House is a colonial gem, which is best appreciated while dining by one of its fireplaces, or perhaps gathering with family and friends for Sunday brunch. However, if it's more than just food and history you're looking for, you probably won't be disappointed—this two hundred and fifty-year-old house just might also have some of the country's oldest ghosts…

MAJOR ANDRE.

There are eyewitness accounts dating back several decades indicating that something of the house's colorful history may still be echoing down its halls and stairways. There was a dishwasher named Baltimore who lived alone upstairs for many years. He would often hear footsteps and voices throughout the house and quickly came to realize that all of this activity did not come from the world of the living. Although terrified by the bold and noisy ghosts, they at least did not enter his room. However, just in case they ever did, Baltimore kept a rope ladder by his window so he could make a quick escape from the house!

66

Over the years, other employees have also heard the footsteps and voices. On at least one occasion, the police were called because it sounded like someone was upstairs after the restaurant had closed, but no one was found. The early morning hours also seem to be popular with at least one ghost who has often been heard coming down the staircase from the second floor—perhaps to get a jump on his day's haunting?

Bobbie Cochran has been the General Manager of the Old '76 House for the past seventeen years, and she believes that the stories about footsteps and voices are true. In addition to her own experiences, employees have told her about feeling a strong presence. Several patrons have heard a strange sound by the front door, as if someone's heels were being dragged across the threshold. Nobody feels comfortable going into the basement alone. There is never anything threatening or harmful, but nonetheless there is credible evidence from many eyewitnesses over a long period of time.

While activity can occur anywhere within the restaurant, if you want a prime paranormal seat, request Table #2. Tablecloths on that table have been seen to move on their own. There was a loud sound of silverware crashing to the floor by Table #2, but when the staff came to see what happened, not a thing was out of place.

Table #2 is by the wall, to the left of the fireplace.

The most common occurrence at Table #2 involves the glass flue. All of the tables are set in colonial style, and each has a candleholder with a glass flue. There has never been any problem with these candleholders, except at Table #2. The glass flue is often found laying on the table or the floor. No one can figure out why the flue repeatedly comes off of its base, or why it hasn't broken when it falls to the floor. No one has actually seen or heard it happen, but just about everyone on the staff has replaced the wandering flue.

The candleholder on table #2.

Just in case you think that this particular candleholder is defective, they have switched it with other candleholders. On a different table, the flue remains in place, but whatever holder is on Table #2 invariably has the same problem!

When I first met with Bobbie in December of 2003, we were sitting at Table #3. She pointed to the candleholder at #2, and explained what happens to it. I looked over, saw that the flue was upright, and then moved on to other questions. About twenty minutes later, Bobbie was summarizing some of the activity she had experienced, and turned to gesture toward the suspicious table, and suddenly stopped speaking. Glancing up from my notes, I saw that she was looking at Table #2 with an odd expression.

There was the flue, laying on the tabletop. No one had gone near the table while we were there, and we didn't hear anything fall. Also, this was not at midnight in an empty restaurant—this was lunchtime, with many other people present. If there are ghosts at the Old '76 House, they certainly aren't shy about being active in broad daylight!

Bobbie has also photographed some strange things. In the lobby by the main entrance, and the adjoining hallway and restrooms, people often feel a strong male presence. One night Bobbie sensed something, and quickly took a few pictures, capturing an inexplicable streak of light in the center of the lobby. She seems to be particularly sensitive to the unusual energies in the Old '76 House—perhaps because of her own unique energy…

This early photo of the open front of the Old 76 House illustrates how close the place came to being completely demolished. Also, some sensitive people have suggested that the activity at Table #2 is the result of it being in the path of a former doorway—an idea that actually is supported by this photograph, which shows that the current location of Table #2 was indeed a doorway.

We went to investigate the restaurant one Monday night in January of 2004. Since I have been finding that people with unusual levels of energy around their bodies often have more frequent paranormal experiences, one of my main objectives in the investigation was not only the restaurant itself, but its general manager, Bobbie Cochran. I set some EMF meters on a table, and asked various members of the staff to sit still near the meters, move their hands close to them, etc. The meters had basically no reaction to the men and women I first tested. Then came Bobbie and the alarms went off, literally! I retested a few people, and again found nothing. Then it was back to Bobbie who sent the meters into a little frenzy of readings.

Everyone's body produces a natural electric field, but there are a few people like Bobbie who have unnaturally strong fields. How this affects or influences the sixth sense is just speculation, but as the energy levels of paranormal events are similar to those of people with personally high levels, it may be something akin to tuning a radio to the right frequency.

Manager Bobbie Cochran with an EMF meter, proving that she has an "electromagnetic" personality.

And speaking of radio—as the restaurant was still open when we began our investigation that night, there was music being piped into all of the rooms. It was some type of jazz, which produced a bizarre atmosphere for a ghost hunt. Normally, we work as silently as possible, so we found it amusing—if not exactly productive—to have the tinkling of the ivories and a wailing sax while we searched for paranormal activity. As you never know what you are going to encounter, you learn to roll with the punches (or the jazz) and make the best of what you have to work with.

Surprisingly, even with the background music, we almost immediately started getting some high EMF readings in the large dining room in the northwest section of the building. Ruling out natural electrical sources, such as the speakers in the ceiling, we still found two areas of interest. There was a spot of high readings near the floor by the outside wall, and one by the fireplace in the back of the room. Perhaps some wiring in the floor or wall could have accounted for the first location, but Mike did get an interesting photo of me measuring the field. The spot by the fireplace also had an added twist—it moved.

When Mike went back to recheck the suspicious area in front of the fireplace, he found that the high readings were now several feet to the left. I don't think we needed an electrician to tell us that wiring doesn't move!

We took a lot of photographs in that room, as well as infrared video. Only one fleeting, tiny object zipped by the video camera, too swiftly to determine what it was. However, in one the photographs, there was a very bright streak of light. (It was similar to the one at Trolley View Farm, see *Ghost Investigator: Vol. 2*.) It was something like a comet

Mike photographed me measuring a high EMF field, and there is an orb above the meter near the ceiling.

with a very bright head and a very dim tail. As everything else in the picture is in focus and the camera was steady, it was only the light that was moving. We tried to reproduce the image to see if there had been some type of reflection, but the mysterious streak appeared in only one of the many photographs.

Close-up of the streak.

The streak of light in the dining room in the northwest corner of the building.

In an adjacent smaller dining area (the one with all of the eagles on the wall), there were some high EMF readings that followed a line, forming something like wall. The field was narrow, and stretched most of the height and length of the room. Whether or not there was some natural explanation, such as electrical lines running through the floor or ceiling, could not be determined—without using a crowbar to pry up some boards, and I didn't think anyone would appreciate that. However, Mike also reported that there was a strange ringing in his ears as he investigated this wall of energy, so it remains an area of interest.

The Eagle Room. An orb is under a table (right) along the line of high EMF readings.

We also examined the basement, and while much of the first two floors of the old Mabie house have been gutted and rebuilt over the centuries, it was fascinating to see the original stone and brickwork that had been put in place when colonists in the area were still wearing wooden shoes.[1]

On the north and south ends of the basement, there are tall brick arches. Speculation by the staff about these arches included former

---

[1] A pair of Dutch wooden shoes was unearthed during construction to an addition of the Old '76 House in 1998. They are in the collection of the Orangetown Historical Museum and Archives. See *Rockland County Scrapbook*, page 6.

Another interesting photo of the Eagle Room. (See hazy patch upper left.)

doorways and brick ovens. I took several pictures of them, not specifically as part of the ghost investigation, but so that they might help me identify what the structures were at some point. When I checked the images, I found that there were some orbs in one photo of the north arch. There weren't any unusual readings at the time, but as this was the only photo displaying the spots of light—and this area is beneath Table #2—it is worth noting.

(A few weeks later, I was able to find a reference that stated that these arches supported the original fireplaces on the first floor at each end of the house. In fact, the fireplace on the north end was quite substantial, as that room was the kitchen when the house was first built.)

We also investigated the second floor. In contrast to the spacious and open first floor, these rooms were small and felt somewhat cramped and confining. I couldn't help but think of poor old Baltimore and his rope ladder, ready to make his escape when the restless spirits walked these floors in the dead of night. While we did not encounter anything unusual there, if I had to sleep in the Old '76 House, I think I would first make sure I knew the way to nearest exit!

74

The arch on the northern end of the basement. A bright spot is on the right edge.

Having gone through almost the entire building from top to bottom, we only had one place left to investigate—Table #2. Unfortunately, as the restaurant neared closing time, only one table remained occupied, #2. For a while, Bob, Mike and I sat patiently in the Eagle Room, where we could see (through the windows in the wall between rooms) the two men and one woman at that table sipping their coffee. (They didn't see us, and had no idea we were waiting for them to leave, or that a ghost investigation was being conducted.)

One of the men and the woman started to stand, so we stood up to prepare to get on with our investigation, but the other man ordered more coffee and all five of us sat down again. About ten minutes later, the man and woman stood up to leave, so the three of us got to our feet, but when their well-entrenched and talkative companion didn't budge, we all reluctantly sat back down. It was like some choreographed vaudeville skit, but it wasn't funny for very long. Closing time came and went, the man had enough coffee to float a battleship, and Bob and Mike began considering using him to recreate the sound of someone's heels being dragged out the front door.

Of course, it's tough to blame anyone for lingering after a fine dinner in such a charming restaurant, but the man's two companions were beginning to look as anxious to go as we were to see them leave. Then the man slowly began to rise, sat back down for a breathless moment, and then finally, mercifully, stood up and put on his coat. As soon as they left, we moved in on that dining room, specifically the area around Table #2. Unfortunately, after all that waiting, we came up empty—no wandering flue, no high readings and no unusual images.

The lobby where a strong presence is felt, and where Bobbie has photographed strange images. There is a patch of light in the upper right corner that may be a reflection, but we could not reproduce it in subsequent photos.

Still, we were certainly not disappointed by our night in the former Mabie house. There were enough anomalies to suggest that something unusual is going on, and with all of the eyewitness accounts stretching over decades, it appears certain that this is one historic building that will carry on its haunted legacy for at least one more century.

Perhaps when the Old '76 House is celebrating its 400th or 500th anniversary, mankind will have finally unlocked the secrets of wandering spirits. By then, we may discover why these ghosts still walk across the creaking floorboards, continue to hold conversations with others who are long dead, and keep leaving little clues to the living that they are not alone here.

In the meantime, don't hesitate to indulge in an excellent meal within the walls that once held Major André prisoner. In fact, it may be his famous restless spirit causing some of the haunted activity, as he still waits for George Washington to grant a pardon and spare him the noose. (Or, it may be the aroma of the delicious pumpkin soup on a cold winter's day that attracts him—because I know it tastes so good it's enough to bring anyone out their grave.)

There are few structures that survive today with the rich history of the Old '76 House, and fewer still that are open to the public. Enjoy the food, appreciate the history, and if you are seated at Table #2 and strange things happen, don't say I didn't warn you!

Spirit Call

"My story is hard for anyone to believe, but I assure you it is absolutely true. To give you the precise details would encompass a novel containing my background and how I got to where I am. For time purposes I will tell you this...up until 14 months ago I did not believe in ghosts, God or 'energy' that would direct my course in life. This has changed completely and totally by the events of the last year."

This is how journalist Steve Banks began to tell his incredible story. Steve grew up on Cromwell Hill Road in Monroe, in Orange County, New York. By his own account, he did not believe in the paranormal, and went about life in an ordinary, practical manner. Unfortunately, that life hit a few rough patches, so he went to see a friend in the Great Smoky Mountains of North Carolina and decided to move there. Steve loved the majestic beauty of the area, and with renewed spirits he planned to make a clean start.

However, you know what they say about the best-laid plans, especially where spirits become involved. Of course, it all began innocently enough. Steve had packed all his things, left Monroe, and headed south. A few hours later, he saw signs for Gettysburg, Pennsylvania. He admits to always having an "attraction" for things regarding the Civil War, so he decided to check out the battlefield.

Anyone who has ever visited Gettysburg will undoubtedly find it amusing that Steve "thought it was a simple field somewhere and nothing more than a history marker would be attached." However, even if you are familiar with the history of the battle, most people (including myself) are very much surprised by the sheer scale of the massive battlefield, and the scores of monuments and historic markers that stretch for miles.

Steve began to grasp the idea when he saw the sign on Route 15 reading, "Gettysburg Battlefield - Next Three Exits." At the time, he believed that he had randomly chosen the second exit, and then made a series of arbitrary turns. However, chance may have had nothing to do with his choices. As dusk painted the Gettysburg landscape into a canvas of twisted shadows among rigid monuments, *something moved*—and it was about to blow the lid off that safe and secure world where everything is normal and has a rational explanation.

"A shadow flitted across the front of my car and my hair stood up on my neck. I followed the shadow to an area of several of these granite markers, where I focused on one. The distinct figure of a uniformed man stood leaning on this particular marker, long and tall like an obelisk. I looked around to see if anyone else was in the area, and then looked back. The shadow man was gone.

I decided to park my car and walk over to the obelisk to see why my eyes had played such a terrible trick on me. As I approached, I was horrified to see the marker was dedicated to "The New York Orange Blossoms," a fighting regiment that came from Orange County, New York, and fought on this spot. They were deemed some of the most valiant Union soldiers under the flag. The marker was erected at the spot where James Cromwell was shot and killed. Cromwell, of Cromwell Hill where I grew up!"

I suppose statisticians would say that the odds of Steve Banks leaving the highway at the second exit, making the series of turns, and then walking straight up to this particular monument would be one in 1,320. That's how many monuments there are in Gettysburg— 1,320—but I doubt that a story like this could be found in another one in a million people.

Yet Steve's story doesn't end here—in fact, it is merely the beginning.

"I went into town and desired to tell this tale to someone...by the time I found my way out of the park it was raining rather hard, after 9pm, and the only store open was a shrewd looking gift shop a few blocks from a McDonalds. I went in and found a gentleman dressed in full Union regalia. His first words to me were, 'You look like you just saw a ghost, son, sit down and tell me about it...' I did so, and he proceeded to tell me a whole bunch of stories of travelers with similar experiences."

79

The inscription on the side of the monument dedicated to the 124th NY—the "Orange Blossoms" regiment—by Devil's Den and the Triangular Field in Gettysburg. At the top it reads, "Killed Major James Cromwell."

This monument still watches over the site where many brave members of the regiment fell on July 2, 1863. The inscription on the back reads, "The Orange Blossoms went into action on this spot with 18 officers and 220 men. Lost in killed and wounded 7 officers and 85 men." That is a casualty rate of 39 percent.

The sign near the 124th NY monument, across from the Triangular Field. A picture of Major Cromwell is in the upper right corner (see enlargement on the next page). The Triangular Field is the site of many paranormal events (see my personal account in *Ghost Investigator: Volume 2*).

Before he left the store, Steve bought a Confederate hat. The owner put the hat in a box, and Steve put it on the back seat of his car, and then attempted to continue his journey. However, a dense wall of fog descended, and he soon found it impossible to continue. He turned around, and immediately saw a sign welcoming him to Gettysburg.

"Almost instantly the fog completely cleared. I turned around again and headed back toward the highway only to hit that wall of fog as soon as I left the city limits."

Finally giving up, he checked into a small motel, hoping he could get some rest after his shocking experience. Then around 3am, his car alarm started wailing.

"I ran out to see who was trying to break into my car only to find the doors locked...then I was spooked again. The rebel hat I had bought was out of the box and on the front dashboard of my car, facing my room. I think I screamed, 'My God!' or something, ran back into my room and suffered through a very light and squeamish sleep. I left abruptly at first light. The hat went into the trunk where it stayed for several months."

Maj. James Cromwell of the 124th New York rode down through the Triangular Field amidst a storm of bullets to rally his men. So gallant did he appear that even some of the Texans shouted, "Don't shoot at him – don't kill him." He and his gray horse fell dead at the bottom of the field.

Steve finally made it to North Carolina without further incident. He moved several times between temporary lodgings, and now lives in a house he is in the process of buying. It is within view of Cold

Mountain (made famous by the recent book and movie), and probably not coincidentally, the farmhouse and land have an interesting history of their own. Steve discovered that they once belonged to a man named Burnette, who fought in the Civil War. In fact, he was known as a skilled sharpshooter, who killed several Union officers at Gettysburg. Major Cromwell was killed at Gettysburg. Could there have been some connection?

"Then one particular night about five weeks ago, I was awakened very late at night to a child's voice calling to me in an extreme southern accent, saying, 'Mister, Mister, wake up...the Yankee Captain is here to see you...'

I awoke in a frightful fit and looked out the window to see the shape of a little girl in a white nightgown motioning me to come outside. It was very dark outside, but I saw her as clear as day. Strange, when I think back I was not as scared as I should have been, I walked to my front door and opened it. The voice was so clear I was sure the little girl was outside...Needless to say, no one was there.

I told my story to a neighbor, of the little girl calling to me in the night...I was told she has been seen regularly by other folks, though I've not met any."

The shadowy figure at Gettysburg with ties to the place where Steve grew up, the farm on which he now lives which was once owned by a man who may have killed Union officers at Gettysburg, the little girl warning of Yankee soldiers—this had become Steve's new reality. He knew he needed answers to all of these bizarre experiences, but there would be one more experience that would prompt him to action.

In late July, he had an intense dream about Major Cromwell, who was asking for help. Steve woke up realizing it was time to do something. He set out to contact someone who wrote ghost books about Gettysburg, and when he conducted an Internet search, he came upon my name and saw that I lived just minutes away from his hometown of Monroe, New York. He sent me an intriguing email, I replied with great interest, and he then shared his remarkable story.

This prompted me to begin researching Major Cromwell. In the first few days, I was able to locate his photograph, and read a detailed account written by the man who accompanied Cromwell's body back to Orange County. And probably not by coincidence, I already had a trip to Gettysburg planned, so that same week I was able to photograph the monument to which the shadowy soldier had lured Steve Banks.

It appears as if one hundred and forty-one years after the guns of the Battle of Gettysburg fell silent, another trigger was pulled. This trigger was to initiate a series of paranormal events that have steered Steve's life in new directions. How will all these pieces of the puzzle fit together? Only time—and the inexorable pull of the spirit's call—will tell.

Clinton Road

I generally only deal with cases that have reliable eyewitnesses and as many verifiable facts as possible. I shy away from the popular tales, urban legends, and that place that "everyone knows is haunted." However, this case is so outrageous, with so many wild and varied claims that I couldn't resist. And who knows—perhaps beneath this mountain of unrealistic stories there might actually be a real ghost or two!

In December of 2003, I was contacted by Michael Kruse, a reporter for the *Times Herald-Record* newspaper in Orange County, NY. Michael wanted to know if I had heard of Clinton Road in West Milford, New Jersey, as he was planning to do a story on it. I was vaguely familiar with the bizarre Clinton Road stories, but had mentally assigned them to the realm of what happens when a car full of drunk teenagers drives down a long, dark road that "everyone knows is haunted."

The reporter was of the same opinion, but he was curious to see if there just might be any scientific evidence behind the stories—evidence that would be best gathered by a ghost investigator. How could I resist?

Before describing what did, and did not, happen that cold evening in December, I must give some background information on this mysterious ten-mile stretch of bad road. The best way to approach this would be simply to list the alleged phenomena.

1. <u>Dead Man's Curve</u>- There is a sharp curve on Clinton Road that is comprised of a bridge between a lake and a creek. Supposedly, a young boy was on this bridge when a car struck him and knocked him into the lake where he died. For many decades, people claimed to have seen the boy's ghost standing on the bridge, as well as his face looking up out of the water. A popular legend says that if you stand on the bridge and throw a coin into the lake, he will throw it back at you.

Dead Man's Curve

2. <u>The Old Lady</u>- There is also supposed to be a ghost of an old lady walking on the side of the road. She seems to be able to stay alongside your car no matter how fast you are going.

3. <u>The Hell Hound</u>- Many people have reportedly been chased by a whitish, wolf-like animal with red or yellow glowing eyes. This animal has supposedly scratched the paint off of cars it has pursued, and also has the ability to run as fast as a car (although it doesn't seem

to be able to catch anyone on foot!). Some people have speculated that this creature was some wild animal that escaped from the nearby Jungle Habitat zoo (no longer open).

4. Satan Worshippers- What story about the deep, dark woods would be complete without Satan worshippers? Actually, there are numerous reports of cult activity in the woods, which if true, would make it far more dangerous than just a place with a few ghosts. Blood, bones and ritual implements have supposedly been found, and anyone trespassing on the rites of these cult members gets chased—or worse.

5. Dismembered Bodies- Which may or may not have anything to do with the last two items. Despite the fact that police records indicate that only one murder victim's body was dumped in these woods in the last several decades, stories persist that bodies are found in the woods around Clinton Road on a regular basis.

6. Ku Klux Klan- The KKK is also supposedly holding meetings and killing people in these woods, or on the island in the lake.

7. Nazis- See the description for item 6.

8. Cross Castle- There was an old abandoned mansion off Clinton Road where Satan worshippers and/or Klan members performed their evil deeds. The building was demolished in 1988, and there were claims that many dismembered bodies were found in the "dungeon" of the castle.

9. A Boy with a Stick- A dirty, barefoot boy with a stick is supposed to chase people through the woods, although opinions differ as to whether or not the boy is a ghost.

10. Albinos- There is also supposed to be one or more albinos who chase people through the woods.

11. Midgets- Yes, also midgets chasing people.

12. Black Pickup Trucks- Ominous-looking black trucks suddenly appear behind you and try to run your car off the road.

13. Nudists- And last, but certainly not least, there are stories of a haunted nudist colony in the woods along Clinton Road.

It sounds to me like these woods are awfully crowded. If even half the stories are true, there must be midgets bumping into Nazis running into nudists tripping over bodies being eating by Hell Hounds being chased by albino boys with sticks every night of the week! But all kidding aside, there continues to be so many eyewitness accounts of strange happenings in this area that *Weird N.J.* magazine actually put out a special issue containing only Clinton Road stories.

Armed with this knowledge, reporter Michael Kruse, newspaper photographer Tony Savino, and I met in Warwick, NY, late one afternoon and prepared for our trip into the unknown. The idea was to examine the road in daylight, then bring out the equipment after dark and see what we could find. My first impression of Clinton Road was that it was in very poor shape, with potholes and crumbling pavement, and trees so close to the road's edge that a driver's slightest mistake could result in an accident.

After several miles we came upon the infamous Dead Man's Curve, which is indeed as dangerous a section of road as you would care to encounter in darkness or bad weather. Anyone driving here for the first time should take extra caution—regardless of whether there are any ghosts. We continued down the desolate road until it abruptly ended at Route 23. The sudden traffic and sight of gas stations, a restaurant and a Dunkin Donuts was quick to break the spell of the spooky Clinton Road.

Turning around, we headed back to Dead Man's Curve, where we stopped this time. While we were tempted to investigate the woods, we decided not to venture far from the cars. This was not out of any fear of rampaging midgets. It was because the state of New Jersey had recently authorized a bear hunt, and it's never a good idea to stroll through the woods when hunters are on the loose.

(A note on the bear hunt: Many of the bears were described as being so docile that they would innocently walk right up to the hunters, who would then shoot and kill them. This is their idea of a sport? People like that are more horrifying than any ghost story...)

The first thing we noticed when we got out of the car was that it was very cold and damp. Bone-chilling cold. Unfortunately, that's one of the things ghost investigators have to contend with, and I did my best to set up the cameras and instruments with rapidly numbing fingers. We took a quick look around, I started taking readings, and Michael tossed a quarter into the lake to see if it would be thrown back. As it was so very, very cold, the lake was frozen and the quarter bounced for a few feet and skidded to a halt, where it remained untouched by ghostly fingers.

I continued looking for any signs of paranormal activity at Dead Man's Curve, while Tony photographed my efforts. The most tense moments came when he asked me to stand in the middle of the curve for a few pictures, which I agreed to do only if he and Michael let me know when any speeding vehicles were headed my way!

"I've officially gotten nothing," Michael quoted me as saying (in the December 21 edition of the newspaper) at the end of the investigation that night. "No orbs. No darting lights. No nothing." There wasn't even so much as a shorter-than-average person threatening us.

As you may have noticed, I have a lot of trouble taking this story seriously, but I also will not say that nothing strange has ever happened on Clinton Road. Despite all of the hype and hysteria, there just may be some kernel of truth to the legends. Perhaps there *are* a few wandering spirits, and maybe some fringe groups *have* used the woods to perform rituals.

If even a tiny percentage of the hundreds of reports about this place are true, then it is well worth your time to take a trip down the dark and lonely road at midnight. Toss a coin in the lake at Dead Man's Curve, venture into the woods and see if you find any bones, and keep your eyes open for misty forms or wolf-like creatures. But above all, be careful, unless you want to add your own tragic story to the frightening tales of Clinton Road.

A few days after writing this story in July of 2004, Bob and I went to Clinton Road to take a few more pictures. The first thing we discovered was that there weren't any road signs at the north end of the road, so unless you know where you're going, you will have to stop and ask directions.

There had just been a few days of heavy rains, and the terrible road surface looked even worse as flooding had washed all kinds of gravel and debris onto the pavement. I can't imagine actually driving on this road when it is flooded, and would further caution readers that while thunderstorms provide great atmosphere for a ghost hunt, they would make Clinton Road even more treacherous. There was one silver lining, or black as the case may be, as several miles of Clinton Road have been recently paved. But don't get too spoiled, as there is plenty of crumbling road surface at each end.

Bob had never been on the road, and he kept joking at even the slightest bend that this must be Dead Man's Curve. He was clearly not taking any of this seriously, but his tune would change as we exited Clinton Road...

The portion of the lake where the boy is supposed to have died, and where people still claim to see his face in the water.

First, we had to stop at the real Dead Man's Curve where I took some pictures, and Bob threw a penny in the lake—it was not thrown back. There are all kinds of graffiti on the barricades and road surface. Obviously, not the brightest people paint these symbols and names, as there were at least two swastikas that were drawn backwards.

As we continued on, I was amazed at how vast and dense the woods really were, as in

The backward swastika and KKK on the road.

December without any leaves they had a totally different character. I would imagine it is easy to get disoriented and lost with such limited visibility. Also, despite the fact that it was a bright, sunny summer's day, it was quite dark in the woods, which undoubtedly adds to the whole mystique of the place.

The dark road past Dead Man's Curve.

As you continue driving south beyond Dead Man's Curve, there is a string of houses, and then the intersection with Route 23. Bob was still joking about the alleged death and destruction of the place, and then as we pulled onto the highway, a huge, speeding SUV came within inches of slamming into us. We both gasped at the extremely close call.

After a few minutes, the shock subsided and I was able to joke about how marvelous an addition this would have been to the legend of Clinton Road—"Ghost Investigator Dies Leaving Clinton Road, Last Photos in her Camera were of Dead Man's Curve!"

Fortunately, tragedy was narrowly averted, and Bob and I did not become statistics of this road. However, it only further emphasized that there were enough manmade and natural dangers here without all of the ghostly and gruesome tales.

If you still feel the need to visit Clinton Road and explore the densely wooded wilderness around it, be prepared for anything, living or dead—and please try to remain in the realm of the living.

One of the road signs warning of the approach of Dead Man's Curve. Someone has painted "DIE" in red on this sign. A "No Trespassing" sign is posted on the tree.

Ghost Briefs

Over the years, many people have come up to me at my lectures and book signings and shared some intriguing stories of their encounters with ghosts. As such events are not conducive to in-depth interviews, I usually ask people to contact me later with more details. Unfortunately, whether due to shyness, lack of time or simply forgetting, all too often I never hear another word. It's a shame, as there is a lot of good evidence going uncollected.

Also, there are often no opportunities to conduct investigations, as the places in question may have been torn down, or have been sold to new owners who don't want to be bothered. Although many of these cases are short on details, I hate to waste any good ghost story.

Therefore, the following consists of some of these brief, but fascinating accounts that I have been accumulating.

West Nyack, New York- An old house near the Four Corners (intersection of Sickletown Road and Nyack Turnpike) was damaged by fire around the turn of the century. Part of the house was then sealed off behind a wall. Several years ago, the family living in the house kept hearing strange music coming from behind that wall, the type of music that would have been played on an old Victrola.

They eventually decided to renovate the house, tore down the wall, and found a furnished room that had been untouched for generations. There was about a hundred years worth of dust on everything in the room, except for one item—an old Victrola that appeared as if it had been recently used!

Walkill, NY- A woman was in the process of selling her house, which included a large barn on the property. As she began removing some items from the barn, she noticed that she was feeling dizzy and had a headache. These particular items had once been used for a rather spirited stallion that had died many years earlier, and the uncomfortable feeling surrounding the area where they were stored progressed into painful electric shocks whenever someone went near. Even the family dog staggered out of the barn one day as if he had been stunned, and refused to go back in there again.

Although the woman had lived on the property for many years, nothing like this had ever happened, and she found it hard to believe that the spirit of this horse would try to harm anyone, as it had been very loving in life.

Curiously, the onset of this shocking activity also corresponded with her decision to sell the weathervane on the barn that had been put there by the previous owner. This man had hit upon hard times, and was going to lose the property. However, before that could happen, he died falling from the roof of the barn. Some say it was an accident as he was working on the weathervane, others believe it was suicide because he was despondent over his financial troubles.

Unfortunately, I don't know if the weathervane was ever sold, or if the new owners have the same shocking experiences.

Haverstraw, NY- A couple moved into an old Victorian house on Route 9W. There were strange noises in the attic, but with a house of that age, it didn't seem too unusual. Then one night the wife, Amy, saw something remarkable in the corner of her bedroom. She emailed me the following account:

"It was two women, one older than the other but neither 'old.' The older one had dark hair and the younger one had lighter hair, not really blonde, but definitely not as dark as the other. I wasn't afraid or intimidated, and I don't even know if they were trying to tell me something, I just got a really nice feeling from them.

My mistake was waking my husband, who thought I had flipped. He turned on the light, then proclaimed, 'There is nothing there.' Obviously if you turn on a light, they are not going to stick around for coffee and cake. This happened a few months ago and I still hear the noises but haven't had the honor of any visitors again."

When I spoke to Amy, she was able to fill in more details. Both women were wearing Victorian style clothing, with high collars and hats. The older woman—around 45-50—wore her dark hair up and was dressed in a fancier dress. The other woman—perhaps in her late teens, and possibly the other woman's daughter?—had blond hair that hung down in more of a child's fashion.

Both were only visible from the waist up and appeared to be sitting, looking directly at Amy. Despite asking her husband not to turn on the light, he did, and the two ghostly figures instantly vanished.

Since that sighting, there has been some odd behavior from an antique Victorian lamp in the living room, which stands directly under the spot where the ladies appeared in the second floor bedroom. Even though all of the other lights in the room never even flicker, this lamp will slowly dim and then get bright again. Amy's husband claims it's a problem with the lamp's wiring, but that lamp is okay when plugged into another socket, and anything else plugged into that particular socket works fine, as well.

Recently, a skeptical friend came to visit. As they sat in the living room, the lamp began its mysterious dimming routine, prompting the friend to ask, "Okay, how are you doing that?" If she was asking Amy, she was asking the wrong person.

What is it about this section of the house? Why have these two phantom women returned, and what message do they want to bring to the world of the living?

Amy is currently researching the history of the house, and recently received some interesting information. While checking some files at the County Clerk's office, an employee asked if she wanted to know the history of her house because she had ghosts. This employee said that many of the houses near where Amy lives are haunted! Apparently, Amy has not been alone in her search for answers about these Victorian homes in Haverstraw.

Hopefully, more evidence will present itself, and more pieces of this puzzle will come together. And if the spirits of these two women do visit again, maybe this time they will stick around long enough for coffee and cake.

Now that's my idea of a civilized way to conduct a ghost investigation!

Haverstraw, NY (Vicinity)- A family living in yet another Victorian-era home was being terrorized by the menacing apparition of a woman in the upstairs hallway. In addition to the dark, ghostly figure, which appeared as if it was trying to cause harm, the family would often hear a terrible crashing sound, as if something heavy had fallen onto the first floor beneath the staircase.

Researching the house's history, they came upon an account where a woman had committed suicide by jumping over the banister of the staircase, falling to her death on the floor below. Unfortunately, this knowledge did not alleviate the haunting. This woman was apparently angry and cruel in life, and death has not softened her personality, or evil intent.

Poughkeepsie, NY (Vicinity)- A woman moved into a house that had a reputation for being haunted, and quickly discovered it was true. If she went out at night, she would always turn on the porch light. When she returned home, the porch light would turn itself off as she walked to the door, as if to imply she was not welcome. The horn of her car would also blow on its own as she walked toward it.

When she was inside the house, the doorbell would ring, although no one was ever there. She had the doorbell checked, and it was found that the wiring in the wall had been cut—so the bell should not have been able to ring at all.

Such frightening things took place in the house, that the woman installed a deadbolt on the inside of her bedroom door. Every night, she bolted herself in before going to bed. Even though she lived alone, and there wasn't any way for anyone to enter her room, on several occasions she discovered strange objects had somehow appeared.

Several times she woke up to find old-fashioned dog collars hanging on the doorknob and wall—inside her room. Another morning, she found that a cane had been hung on the wall as she slept.

The woman moved out, and the place became a Bed & Breakfast. I wonder if they allow dogs?

Poughkeepsie, NY- Several people have told me about The Country Manor restaurant on Route 55. There is supposedly the ghost of an elderly man wearing a gray sweater walking around inside. He has appeared for many years, and been seen by many different eyewitnesses. Several waitresses have allegedly quit after seeing the spirit of the old man. I called the restaurant a few years ago, and the person I spoke to confirmed that although he had never had any encounters, he knew people who had seen the ghost.

Jersey City, NJ- An older woman who worked as a nurse lived in a house that had many strange sounds. She would also often encounter an intensely foul odor for which she could find no explanation. One night when her uncle was visiting, she told him that she believed the place was haunted. He laughed at the idea—until just a few seconds later, when pieces of the ceiling fell down right on top of him!

The most bizarre thing occurred with an old family sword that was displayed on the mantel. The woman noticed that there was red liquid on the blade. She cleaned it off, but later discovered it had reappeared. Being a nurse, she thought that the liquid resembled blood, but how could that be? Finally, she took a sample of the red liquid from the sword and had it analyzed. Tests proved conclusively that the substance was blood!

Update on Grandma's House

For those of you who read the fascinating story of "Grandma's House" in *Ghost Investigator: Volume 3*, the story continues. In fact, on a recent investigation I had what just might be the most startling experience of my ghost hunting career.

As a brief refresher, this house in Port Jervis, New York, belongs to Mike Worden's grandmother, and for generations people have been experiencing bizarre things—not the least of which is the appearance of a ghost who resembles a former owner. As Mike had been spending more time at the house with his new twin boys, he was able to see firsthand how the activity has increased. Perhaps the babies have stirred up the energies in the place?

While inexplicable noises have become commonplace, one night Mike got more than an earful. He was spending the night in the back bedroom, and something awakened him. He went down the hall to the bathroom, but his attention was drawn back to his bedroom. Turning, he saw the dark figure of a man standing at the other end of the hall. The figure seemed to realize that it had been seen, as it suddenly rushed into his bedroom. Mike ran into the room, but no one was there.

We decided to conduct yet another investigation in the summer of 2004. Mike and I were setting up the equipment upstairs in the front bedroom, while Bob was watching the video monitor downstairs in the living room. (Mike ran cables from the camcorder to the monitor so we could view what was happening without disturbing the scene.) Before we could finish setting up, there was a loud knocking sound behind us.

Bob asked why we were knocking on the wall. That was a question Mike and I didn't want to hear, because we had been hoping that Bob had made the sounds! I told him it wasn't us, he asked if I was kidding, and I said unfortunately I was not. Of course, as personally unsettling as this was, from a paranormal standpoint this was good news, but would the knocking continue?

The sound appeared to emanate from the wall behind us, so I looked out the window just to make sure nothing was hitting the house, like a branch. However, there were no trees, no loose wires, nothing that could have hit the outside of the house at that point.

The old house has solid plaster walls, which feel as hard as a rock. Still, I had to consider the idea that perhaps some animal had gotten into the wall and was making the sounds, although it clearly sounded like a sharp banging, not a scratching or scurrying sound as might be produced by a squirrel.

As I placed my open hands against the wall to test its structural integrity, I thought that what I needed was to hear the knocking again to determine its nature. Something must have read my mind…

Several sharp knocks sounded in the wall beneath my hands, strongly enough that I could feel the vibration. Jumping back a step, I called to Mike. He came out of the bedroom and I told him what had just happened. He had clearly heard the knocking, too, and I asked him if he thought I should try knocking back. We both shrugged our shoulders as if to say, "Why not?" and I stepped forward again. Taking a deep breath, I raised my fist up to the wall and knocked twice.

Instantly, there were two loud knocks in reply!

I admit it, this time I jumped back several feet, and said a few choice words. My eyes were wide, my heart was pounding and my brain was having difficulty processing the sounds that had just been created in response to my knocking. Mike was in a similar state of shock, but I had to ask the question. Should I do it again? We both agreed that was what we were there for, so somehow I found the courage to step back to the wall.

This time, just to be sure that whatever it was had responded specifically to my two knocks, I decided to just knock once. Reaching forward once again, my fist made one quick rap against the hard wall.

Immediately, one sharp rap answered me back!

Life changed for me in that split second, that brief instant where some unseen force directly communicated and responded to me. I have heard phantom footsteps, seen doors opening, witnessed and photographed many strange things, but I knew right then and there, that this was an experience I had never known before. It was intense, it was specific, it was unquestionable, and it was personal.

I knocked twice and something knocked back twice. I knocked once and something knocked back once. This was no muffled voice on tape, no amorphous blob of light in infrared. This was an in-your-face response to my actions, and it was both thrilling and terrifying. This is what a ghost investigator lives for.

An infrared image of Mike standing by the section of the wall where the knocking occurred.

We quickly set up all the cameras and instruments around this wall, but whatever was there had gone. We all tried knocking on the wall again, but whatever it was, had proved its point and had moved on. Although later that night we did record and photograph more of the usual paranormal activity that takes place in that house, the main event was over.

However, activity has continued to increase since then. Mike recently emailed me the following account:

"Just a few days ago one of the boys woke up around 3:30 am. I went in and gave him a bottle. I stood outside the door for a moment to make sure that he stayed settled (one awake twin is not as bad as two!) and while I was standing there I could hear something walking around at the foot of the steps, then what sounded like banging noises...like an object being struck against a table. I peeked over the railing and continued to hear the walking...which went to the stairs. I headed back towards my room and stopped at the top of the stairs. There was minimal light, but no one visible...yet there were footfalls coming up the stairs and the creaking of the railing...and even more creepy - there was a tapping sound along the wall adjacent to the stairs that followed along with the footsteps...it was as if someone was walking up the stairs and tapping the wall along the way!"

That wall just happens to be the same wall where we heard the knocking.

I'm sure this will not be the last update on this house. Things are now occurring on an almost daily basis to all members of the family. Mike's grandmother has now taken to yelling at the entities to be quiet when they make noise in the middle of the night, so that she can get some sleep. I cringe at the thought of the night that they start yelling back!

To order books, get info, and share your haunting,
contact the Ghost Investigator through:

www.ghostinvestigator.com

Or write to:

Linda Zimmermann
P.O. Box 192
Blooming Grove, NY 10914

Or send email to:

lindazim@frontiernet.net

Copy this page to use for your own ghost hunt. If you know of a haunted site you think should be considered for an upcoming book, please contact me at:

P.O. Box 192, Blooming Grove, NY, 10914

www.ghostinvestigator.com

Field Report

Date: Location:

Time In: Weather:

Names of People Interviewed:

Equipment: Camera   ☐Video   ☐Tape Recorder
              ☐ Thermometer   Other:

Experiences: Sounds ☐   Odors ☐   Cold Spots ☐

Visuals ☐Touch/Sensations ☐Movement   ☐

Details (Attach extra sheet if necessary):

Time Out: Total Time on Site:

Conclusions:

Prepared and Signed by:

Witness(es):

Other books by Linda Zimmermann

Ghost Hunter Novel

Dead Center

When one of the country's largest shopping centers is built in Virginia, rumors abound that the place is haunted by ghosts of Civil War soldiers. Ghost hunter Sarah Brooks must uncover the truth, and come face to face with the restless spirits that walk through the *Dead Center* :

Okay, Sarah Brooks. This is what you do, she said to herself. *This is who you are.*

Closing her eyes, Sarah spun around and counted to three. When she opened her eyes, she had to clamp her hand over her mouth to stifle a scream. There was a pale, misty shape of a man drawing closer. It was like an image being projected into a fog, and it rippled, wavered, then slowly began to take on a more defined shape. The wounded man behind her screamed as if Death himself was coming to take him…

Science Fiction Novels *

Mind Over Matter

Ten wealthy, powerful members of the Upper Circle rule the Union with an iron fist, and a small chip implanted in every citizen. Born to the privileged class, Walter Danan is now a wanted man. He has discovered extraordinary powers with which he hopes to break the council's grip and set mankind on a higher path of *Mind Over Matter.*

"Classic space opera!" Ernest Lilley, Editor, *SFRevu*

Home Run

On the fast track to becoming a baseball superstar, Rick Stella's injury leads him to join the Pioneer program for a year-long mission. Pioneers are sent into the farthest depths of space to start colonies, and are often never heard from again.

When Rick becomes marooned with his android crew, he must decide whether he is willing to sacrifice his dreams, or risk everything trying to make it home.

"Linda Zimmermann shows why she's an All-star in combining a story about baseball & SF to remind us how to overcome obstacles to emerge a winner!" Tony Tellado, _Sci-Fi Talk_

History

**Civil War Memories** "An exciting compilation of vignettes which bring Civil War history alive." Alan Aimone, USMA West Point

**Forging a Nation** "Linda Zimmermann blends the history of a single family with the history of our nation in its formative years. This is a story of patriotism, privilege and tragedy which touches the heart, and gives the reader a fascinating and very personal window into the past." William E. Simon, former U.S. Secretary of the Treasury

"A worthy book." Arthur Schlesinger, Pulitzer Prize winning author/historian

Ghost Investigator
Volume I
Hauntings of the Hudson Valley

Revised and updated true stories previously published in:

Ghosts of Rockland County
Haunted Hudson Valley
Haunted Hudson Valley II
Haunted Hudson Valley III

Readers' reviews from Amazon.com :

"If you live in the Hudson Valley area and you like true ghost stories, these books are a must have!"

"I had goosebumps the whole time and I was scared to go to sleep."

Ghost Investigator Volume 2
From Gettysburg, PA to Lizzie Borden, AX

Ghost Investigator Volume 3

"If you really want to get the feeling of what it's like to actually go 'ghost hunting' in cemeteries, cellars and abandoned buildings, you will love this book."

"Linda Zimmermann's books are among the most frightening I've read."

Printed in the United States
21578LVS00004B/1-129